P23 -24
P 31

LEARNING TO READ

LEARNING TO READ

A Guide for Teachers and Parents

by

BRENDA THOMPSON
B.Sc.

SIDGWICK & JACKSON

LONDON

First published 1970
Copyright © 1970 Brenda Thompson

SBN 283 48422.5

Printed in Great Britain by
C. Tinling & Co. Ltd., London and Prescot
for Sidgwick and Jackson Limited
1 Tavistock Chambers, Bloomsbury Way
London, W.C.1

Contents

CONTENTS

Introduction

What is this book about? What it is not about is a new method or mystique of reading. It does, however, put the emphasis where it belongs, with the children . . . It shows reading to be a 'natural' ability like speaking one's native language. In the way that children learn to talk, by talking, so they should learn to read by reading – and more reading. Reading is then to be seen not as a mechanical end in itself, but as the central part of early education, bringing the child in touch with the widest possible range of interesting and appealing material.

When you look at things from the point of view of the children, as I have tried to do in this book, you see they are getting a raw deal. You see their boredom with stale reading schemes accepted as a necessary part of learning. You see their interest in television and comics treated as a barrier to the 'correct' acquisition of literacy. You see their failures knowingly attributed to 'a broken home', 'a poor environment', or to their race, or to their being generally 'deprived'.

What I am saying quite simply, is yes, children are being deprived at the moment, firstly of good and interesting 'readers' and secondly of an atmosphere in which a fluent reading vocabulary is allowed to count for more than a grim, word-by-word battle through the primer.

I should be pleased if my message was found to be obvious to all right-thinking people. However, the actual situation is disturbing and shows no sign of improvement. That is why I believe this book is timely. It mounts an attack on the inept material put out by a lot of educational publishers, on the narrow approach of some teachers, on well-meaning but irrelevant 'solutions' like the Initial Teaching Alphabet (I.T.A.), on the general lack of respect for the customers – our children.

A few weeks after I started teaching I dropped the narrow, conventional way of teaching reading I had been shown, and went off to get the children some good books. I believe many teachers and parents are as dissatisfied as I was then, about the subject of reading, and will find my experience of interest and value.

In this book I have tried to describe the place of reading in the modern infants classroom. I have taken a critical look at the range of reading schemes that are available and the thinking behind them. Then I have gone on to deal with the repertoire of methods an infants teacher must develop to handle the varied problems that arise when children are learning to read. I have evaluated various scientific tests of reading ability. I have put forward practical suggestions for stimulating and maintaining children's interest in reading. I have drawn up lists of recommended books, which I hope will be helpful to both teachers and parents. I also hope that throughout my book I have been able to suggest something of the pleasure and reward there is in teaching children to read.

1 The place of reading

The revolution in the classroom

Every parent expects that one of the first things his child is going to do when he starts school, is to learn to read. Whatever new methods may have come to the infant classroom, the teaching of reading is still seen as the central classroom activity.

Most parents are aware of the revolution that has taken place in recent years in primary education. It is a revolution that is still going on. It has affected the look and layout of the classroom, and almost everything that goes on in the classroom. Small children no longer come to school to sit at desks all day, to be instructed as a class in the rudiments of learning, with perhaps an occasional break to play with plasticine or to do a few physical jerks. Over the past generation we have seen a gradual movement towards more dynamic, informal teaching with greater emphasis on individuals. The so-called 'activity method' – where the child was allowed a certain period of creative activity, followed by a session where he would more formally read and write about his creative period, has blossomed into what is now termed the 'integrated day'. As yet the integrated day is found mostly in infants schools and is really more of an extension of the type of teaching found in nursery classes. It depends upon children having the freedom to follow their own devices but with continual guidance and discreet direction from the teacher.

Although not every school is completely informal, most

schools are informal to some extent, and the chief expression of this as far as parents are concerned, is the large amount of time that children spend in play. In fact some parents are puzzled and upset by this. They want to see their children spending as much time as possible in school in learning and getting on. For such parents one of the tests is how quickly their children learn to read. The informal method seems a threat to this accomplishment. On the other hand all teachers and enlightened parents would agree that, to children, the advantage of a carefree atmosphere is enormous, and that children can learn and develop very well through play. One of the main reasons is that a young child's span of concentration on any subject is extremely short. If he is free to change what he is doing as he feels like it, he is unlikely to become frustrated and bored with school work.

On the face of it, all this might sound merely fashionable permissiveness. It could be argued that if children are kept in their places, they can be more easily observed and more carefully assessed by the teacher, and kept more firmly to the task in hand. However, there is a practical justification of a freer system. Anyone who has spoken to an audience knows that people can switch off quite easily when they have had enough. Children are no exception, and soon begin to fidget and fool about. Also children share with soldiers the knack of making small tasks occupy them for an extremely long time. Given a set task, such as copying a line from a blackboard, children are quite capable of spending an entire morning over it. So if there were no other positive benefits to an informal approach, it should be recognized that a child is likely to be happy at school, and usefully employed, more of the time, than in the old-fashioned classroom.

No new look for reading

Planned informality imposes a great burden on an infants teacher, but the reward is the greater opportunity to see individual skills and talents blooming, often in unlikely places. This is true of reading ability, but it is disappointing that in many respects, reading materials and methods, and teachers' outlooks on the teaching of reading, have not quite kept pace with the major classroom trends. There is a startling contrast between a main!· conventional approach to reading and the new approach to the teaching of mathematics. The New Maths has attracted a great deal of publicity, and no doubt it is what springs to mind when parents hear about the revolution in the classroom. The idea of New Maths has been universally accepted, perhaps because it has been skilfully presented in magazines, newspapers, and lectures. Perhaps for most people mathematics still remains a mystery, and they are willing to give a new teaching philosophy a chance. In doing this they are accepting a philosophy whereby infants do not sit carrying out sums, but learn about mathematical concepts and logical relationships through their play activities. The whole field of mathematics has been expanded. We used to have a situation of pure manipulation of numbers, when children, as we now know, would do sums by means of formulae, without understanding in any way what they were doing. Quite young children are now introduced to concepts of geometry, algebra, and statistics, which they once would not have been thought ready for until their teens.

This exciting development has perhaps overshadowed the teaching of reading. In any case reading seems so obviously within everybody's reach that the methods used for teaching reading are of much less interest to laymen. Reading has not been given a new look and teachers have not been given any guidance as to how it fits into the scheme of an informal classroom.

'Why are you filling his head full of prehistoric animals?'

Is there perhaps a danger when children are encouraged to learn at their own rate, when they are working and playing all over the place, in a continuous hubbub of activity and creativity, that the teaching of reading can become neglected and that the old methods will no longer suffice? How then do we apply to the teaching of reading, the same thinking we have given to mathematics, physical development, and creative skills? We have

11

first of all to take a critical look at the existing material and methods, and the existing attitudes of teachers, educationists, and parents, in order to see what new materials and adaptations are necessary. I do not, however, see reading merely as another subject. I see it as the key subject which is the basis of all education. I think parents are right to feel anxious about their children's reading progress. If a child is not making progress in learning to read, a parent is inclined to blame the system. In this respect there is a crucial difference between the modern classroom and the formal classroom which it replaced. When a child sat in his appointed place with his books and his pencil and paper, the system was visibly in operation. Even if the exercises were sterile, the evidence was unmistakable that if the child was not mastering the art of reading, then at least the teacher and the system and the apparatus were not to blame. Now parents can no longer be sure where the blame lies if something goes wrong. Take the example of a parent who arrives regularly with a complaint that her son has not yet learned to read. 'Why are you filling his head full of prehistoric animals and not teaching him to read?' This mother cannot accept that although her son is not yet capable of learning to read, he is at least more profitably employed studying prehistoric animals, than in sitting resentfully copying words from a blackboard or a card. This boy will learn to read as he gets older. Meanwhile he is applying his intelligence and enthusiasm to learning a great deal about all sorts of subjects. Most important, he chooses and uses books for reference, with assurance and pleasure.

The confident use of language and books is essential in modern education, for we are in an age where the pace of expansion of knowledge is so fast it is impossible to learn every fact. We can learn how to find out what we want or need to know. Books for reference are going to play an increasingly important part in our educational system. When a child has learned to read, his reading can gradually be directed into self-education by finding things out in books, and by following up suggestions and ideas in books.

We widen our horizons and expand our general knowledge when we read. In writing, people put forward ideas and experiences which we absorb and make our own.

Of all the means of communication reading gives us the greatest choice. We can be much more selective in what we read than in what we view, for instance. There is an enormous range of reading material from shops and libraries where we can make our own choice. Television stations are restricted to what programme planners and mass audiences decide upon. Films and theatre also offer a much more limited choice. Reading will remain for some time to come, the most personal and the most efficient source of our information.

2 Methods and techniques

Starting to read

Children learn to walk and talk naturally and mostly by themselves. Learning to read is one of the first major skills they acquire which needs the direct and planned help of an adult. Nonetheless the pattern of learning to read follows an 'S shaped curve' in the same way that learning to speak does. The child at first can deal only with a few words, gradually there is a steep increase in the speed of learning as the child gains a wider vocabulary at a faster and faster rate. Finally when the child has a working knowledge of most of the commonly used words in the language the rate of learning begins to level off. In the very early stages the teacher must use a mechanistic approach, for example pointing out words which the child repeats. When children have acquired enough words to read simple books, the mechanistic approach can give way to one which allows the child the freedom to build a large vocabulary from the context of his reading and from the constant and varied repetition of words that he comes across.

Some teachers persist with the mechanistic phase for too long, insisting, for example, that a child should learn the vocabulary of a new book before he is allowed to handle it, let alone read it. This can only hold a child back and more than likely dampen his enthusiasm. Over-keen adherents of the mechanistic way of teaching reading can go as far as training left-right eye movements. This can sound impressive and plausible to a layman or a student teacher. To a skilled practising teacher it is at best something quite incidental, and at worst something of a joke. If the teacher reads with the children, or to the children, pointing to the sequence of the words along the line, and the sequence of line upon line and page upon page, this order comes just as naturally to a child as walking forwards rather than backwards. Just how implicit all of this is, was brought home to me with the case of a Chinese girl who, although she made excellent progress in reading, would at first insist on turning over the pages of a book backwards, constantly going over the same ground. It is a severe criticism of the available early reading books, that she was at first unaware that she was re-reading the same stuff. Only when I gave her material with a good story line, i.e. a logical sequence, did she get over this confusion.

There are three ways of setting a child off to read. Firstly he can build up an initial working vocabulary from flash cards. These are cards which carry a single word. The teacher shows it to the children and they repeat it until they have learned it. Similarly the teacher can point to a word in a wall caption or a wall story, and the children say it until they have learned it. Thirdly, the child can have very simple caption books from which to learn basic words. Once a minimum starting vocabulary has been gained, a child can go on to reading books of graded difficulty. The amount of help then needed from the teacher varies with each child. In general however, the more a child practises the faster he will learn. He learns in fact, by reading and more reading.

In addition to general 'know how' that the teacher acquires in helping children learn to read, there are a number of recognized methods and techniques for which their adherents make special claims. I shall later examine each of these methods in turn, to see which aspects of reading they emphasize, and how they tackle the general problem.

'Reading Readiness'

The burning questions asked by teachers and parents are,

when is a child ready to read, and how do we recognize that moment? A great deal of thought has been given to this problem of reading readiness, and unfortunately a great deal of nonsense has been talked and written about it. Obviously it would be of the greatest value if a teacher knew well enough not to push a child before he had reached the stage of reading readiness. Sadly there does not seem to be such a magic moment, nor a means of spotting it, if it does exist. Some children need pushing or encouraging. Some children want to try and often make desperate attempts to learn to read like their classmates, long before they are intellectually able. This can be very touching and sad to the teacher. I had a young boy who blamed me and expressed this blame by drawing a lion, which would eat me up for failing to teach him too read. As far as I can judge, the turning point in learning to read is when a child, soon after meeting words, can recognize the same words in another context. Yet it is difficult to make any rules. A child may well recognize the names of the characters in the reading series, or a noun like 'aeroplane' over and over again, but fail to recognize words such as 'the' and 'and'. Yet he may be ready to have a reading book and to go on and acquire words that to him are more difficult, such as 'the' and 'and', from the context. Some teachers may decide that a child is ready to have his first reading book only when he has a complete knowledge of the words in it. This may be correct or it may be too cautious, but sometimes it can lead to disappointment when a child is unable to make any progress to the second book, because the words have been rather too inculcated, with not enough emphasis placed upon the sequence of reading, as opposed to individual words learned parrot-fashion. In the end it comes down to the teacher's intuition and good sense, based upon experience and observation. It is a difficult problem for beginning teachers who will inevitably make mistakes. With the help of a good headmistress and her colleagues, and minimum dependence on fixed rules, the new teacher should quickly acquire the necessary judgement.

It is a good idea to begin to read at the earliest possible age, since a child's general education is mostly dependent on his ability to read and write. A great deal of his general knowledge will be derived from books. There is a very strict limit to what he can be told by a teacher. Today in primary school there is much more emphasis on finding out and recording than on sitting and listening to a teacher's lecturing. From a practical point of view, with classes of forty, and children all learning at different speeds, it is very important for a child to be able to read and get on alone, at his own speed, as soon as he can. Many children are not ready to start reading till six or even later, and this often gives rise to needless anxiety in parents, who think their child is wasting time at school, or who compare him unfavourably with a friend or sibling who could read at the same age. A slow start at reading does not necessarily mean lack of intelligence or poor teaching.

Perhaps the most important single factor which decides the age at which a child will read is the ability to concentrate. Many an intelligent child is slow to start reading because he has poor ability to concentrate. This is particularly true of boys. Boys who enjoy an active physical life, who love rough and tumble, may find sitting quietly and reading or writing, a great strain. Some girls, especially tomboys or ebullient personalities, experience the same difficulty. It is wrong to force them so that they grow to dislike reading and writing. It is however possible to capture their attention with suitably exciting or interesting reading material. The most important thing is for reading and writing to remain a pleasure.

Parents of highly active children should not despair. These may well pass their quieter brothers and sisters as they grow older and their powers of concentration grow. Parents frequently report that their little daughter is cleverer than their little son. This is due to the quieter nature of girls and unfortunate comparisons should not be made as frequently their little sons catch up and even overtake their sisters. Some parents blame the child, some blame the teacher.

Emotional readiness in reading is closely bound up with

concentration. Some children may well be able to sit down and concentrate on quiet work such as drawing a picture or making a model or even doing mathematical work. Yet they may not be able to sit quietly and read. This is probably because they find reading boring. It is very important to find the right kind of reading material to hold the child's attention. The choice will depend on his intellectual ability, his general knowledge, his cultural background. Generally speaking a child who does not enjoy reading for reading's sake will respond to a funny or exciting book. Adults who find themselves with a boring book usually give it up, so why should not a child? Many children's reading books are downright boring.

Some children are not intellectually ready to read in infant school. Some of these children may try very hard to read as they do not like to feel left out. Here remedial classes can help, as also can some attempt at 'pot-boiling' by the teacher in order to save the child's face. Those who are not able to read in infants school and do not particularly want to, must be taught in the junior school. For this purpose close liaison should be kept between the infant and junior classes.

Once the child is seen as being ready to read, how does the teacher build upon that readiness? What methods and techniques are available? Different methods emphasize different factors of the reading problem.

Look and say

The factors that make up 'reading' are:

(1) the appearance of words
(2) the sound of words
(3) the arrangement of words
(4) the meaning of words
(5) the impact of words

The problem that is obvious to everybody is the difference in English between the appearance and the sound of words, a difficulty which does not arise in some other languages, German for example. The way English is written reflects the way it was spoken by certain people some hundreds of years ago. In fact standardized spellings are comparatively recent. Even today there are differences in local spellings. For example, the same words are spelt differently in Britain and America. Most of the techniques that have been developed are obsessed with this problem and keep more than half an eye on the eventual necessity of correct spelling. Thus the 'look and say' method tries to overcome difficulties of recognition by emphasizing the shape or pattern of words. 'Phonics' attacks the problem by showing how letters convert into sounds, and the 'Initial Teaching Alphabet' goes one better by inventing a provisional phonetic language which postpones the spelling problem all together.

'Look and say' is currently the most popular method of teaching reading and likely to be the most successful, probably because it is the most flexible. The principle of 'look and say' as the name implies consists in the child looking at a word and saying it, usually with the aid of a 'flash card' until the word becomes naturally part of his vocabulary. Strict adherents of 'look and say' require a child to recognize all the words in a book before he begins to read it. This is logical but in practice quite unnecessary. 'Look and say' is quite a good method, at least to start the child reading, because there are no restrictions on the vocabulary as in the older phonic method, which was restricted to three-letter words. Of course the main advantage of 'look and say' is that the child is remembering the whole word naturally and not synthesizing it from its components. Unfortunately learning words in isolation is a pointless activity to many children and the difficulty is increased with abstract words.

The word pattern approach may be explained diagrammatically as follows:

A word has a shape thus: house . However, other words will have a similar shape, e.g. horse here down tree but it is claimed these words are not so easily confused as let us say them that they .

19

F. J. Schonell, the influential author of 'The Psychology and Teaching of Reading' suggests that words such as; 'all', 'one', 'eye', 'ate', (all of different patterns although of the same length) are more easily confused than words of varying length such as, 'said', 'Fluff', 'Mother', 'sixpence', 'elephant'. A much more probable reason for the easier recognition of the second set is their evocative nature. Both 'Fluff' and 'Mother' are leading characters in Schonell's reading scheme and any parent must know what a 'sixpence' and an 'elephant' mean to a small child compared to 'all', 'one', eye', or 'ate'.

Schonell goes on to point out the importance of 'ascenders' and 'descenders' in words. Ascenders are letters of which the shape goes above the body of the word, such as $\overline{b}, \overline{d}, \overline{f}, \overline{h}, \overline{k}$, and descenders are letters which drop below the body of the word e.g. $\underline{g}, \underline{j}, \underline{p}, \underline{q}$. By giving two sentences where certain letters have been replaced by 'x' Schonell seeks to prove that the more distinguishable patterns formed when only ascenders and descenders are retained, is more meaningful than when only the descenders and ascenders are replaced with 'x'. What he does not prove is that anyone actually sees words in this way. The shape of words, while important, is only part of the ambiguity that faces a child trying to read an unfamiliar text. The aim must surely be to avoid the child attacking it as a code and to make sure that all the cues are helpful. The word shape idea is quite useful but it has been overstressed, owing to the lack of good reading theory and experimental evidence.

What we do not know about 'look and say' in general is whether the method presents an insurmountable hurdle for certain kinds of children, whose perceptual mechanism may not allow them to make the jump from the whole form of the word to the meaning. There is a hint of this in the fact that a handful of children in a class may learn to write before they ever learn to read because they are able to build up words from sounds.

'Look and say' must be the most ancient method of teaching reading. The early picture languages and hieroglyphics could have used no other method. There are in Chinese, for example, thousands of characters that must be learned individually. Although English is a phonetic language, we know it is rather inefficiently so. Therefore 'look and say' is the easiest and most natural way of starting to read. The supreme advantage is that there need be no restriction on the vocabulary. It can be made as interesting as you like. The classic example is the use of the word 'aeroplane', which is phonetically difficult but is the most easily learned word in the twenty-seven initial words of the 'Janet and John' series, simply because it is such an exciting and intriguing word.

We must distinguish between the formal method of 'look and say' and the automatic looking and saying which goes on anyway when a child is allowed to read on his own. The formal method is likely to make use of flash cards. Once children start to develop at different rates the teacher has to use the flash cards virtually on an individual basis. Teachers find this far too time-consuming and are reluctant to extend formal 'look and say' beyond the very early stages. This is a practical difficulty but fortunately a child can learn to read directly from the primer without the use of flash cards. Another formal approach is to ask the child to 'prepare' a page of reading, that is to recognize the individual words and spot new words. It is the more commonly used method with more advanced children. This is bound to be tedious and is unnecessarily methodical if, as all these schemes claim, the introduction of new words and the repetition of words is planned and graded, and if, as we maintain, there will be a great deal of natural repetition. There are other aspects of the formal teaching of 'look and say', such as word matching, where the children are required to match separate word or sentence cards to a text or picture. There is a variety of such aids-to-reading accompanying the published reading schemes. They represent rather unnecessary variations on a monotonous theme. Children do not particularly enjoy using them and many teachers will find that they smack of commercial over-exploitation. Aids of this type need to be supervised to be effective and the time could be better spent in hearing reading.

What obviously happened was that people observed children learning to read and saw them actually 'looking and saying' as they learned. Thus 'look and say' was erected into a method as an apparently realistic alternative to the abstract approach of phonetics. It cannot properly be called a method but only the external part of what happens when children learn to read. It is going to be something of a mystery until we know much more about how learning and memory work, and particularly about the important role that intuition appears to play in learning and problem-solving.

Reading in context

In the light of this it seems to me that the only reasonable and efficient way to learn to read is through reading in context. This means encouraging a large volume of reading, without troubling too much about accuracy, and reading in a variety of contexts, so that words and meanings are seen from many angles. This is why it is best to start reading with whole sentences or phrases and not single words. A sentence can make immediate sense to a child because it is a statement about something. With the exception of nouns, isolated words tend not to make sense to a small child. Abstract words in particular are extremely difficult. Words regarded as essential in the first lists such as 'the', 'this', 'of', 'for', 'here', have no intrinsic meaning whatsoever. However the frequent repetition of these linking words in context makes for ease of reading.

When a child has acquired a basic vocabulary for the early books in a reading scheme, there should be nothing to stop the growth of reading ability by a snowballing process. Provided that the new words are not introduced too rapidly, the child will assimilate them from the context. The snowballing effect occurs chiefly because children have the ability to make intelligent guesses at new words. This, believe it or not, is often disparaged as a fault.

Of course, guessing will be inadequate in the type of literature such as Janet and John, the context of which is vacuous and inane. Good context provides plenty of clues for good guesses. Wrong guesses are subject not only to the teacher's correction but to correction in context later on. Even fluent adult readers continue to increase and modify their reading vocabulary. Mostly this comes from encountering new words in context and establishing their meaning from the context. Adults do not read with a dictionary beside them. We never stop learning to read (or it might be truer to say that people who read never stop learning to read).

My argument is reinforced by the errors children make when they have to deal with early reading books. They often misread a word because by doing so they make more colloquial sense of the text, or they add a word which to them is obviously missing. For example 'The dog has the ball' becomes 'The dog has got the ball'. 'Mother' frequently becomes 'Mummy'.

' "See the ship out there"
Janet saw the boat'.

becomes

' "See the ship out there"
Janet saw the ship' (from 'Out and About' page 36).

Phonics

The phonic method which relies on teaching sounds in order to build up three letter words, and then larger ones, seems to have fallen out of use as a starting method. This is chiefly because the reading material needed is restricted and tedious. Most children are capable of becoming fluent readers without any phonic teaching. This does not rule out the possibility that some children might be helped by phonics. Just how many and in what way is impossible to say without thorough experimentation, and yet it is difficult to contemplate children being used as guinea pigs. Most teachers teach phonics at some stage, if only to salve their own conscience. It is possible that some children could be hindered by phonics from the apparent need to analyse words, especially those they have already learned and taken for granted. Nonetheless phonics has come to be treated as a supplement to 'look and say' because it introduces a certain amount of order into a potentially chaotic situation.

It is true that phonics are an aid to early writing. Those children that grasp phonics early can work out their own spellings. Those that do not may take longer to learn to write. Phonic spelling of course is often wrong spelling. Just how serious bad spelling is, is debatable. Clearly the more children read and are exposed to words, the better their spelling will tend to be. Early phonetic mistakes in spelling soon correct themselves. Often teachers worry too much about bad spelling, especially in districts where the children's speech is even further from the written form of the language than standard spoken English. Needless to say children get discouraged if their ingenious spelling efforts are criticized. The whole matter raises a dilemma. Should the teacher use phonics to assist early writing at the risk of bad spelling, in order to allow early written expression, or should the teaching of phonics be deferred until the child is a fairly fluent reader, and hopefully, spells with accuracy from memory? Personally I would rather see children writing, however bizarre the spelling, and this is my justification for teaching phonics.

I do not believe that phonic teaching should be laboured. Phonic drill is tedious. It is also very confusing from the start. The teaching of phonetic rules is bedevilled by the need to cater for innumerable exceptions. If one concentrated on the rules the exceptions would logically have to be screened from the rules, and if one considered all the exceptions the speed of learning phonics would fall behind the speed of learning to read. Indeed it does. Once you have accepted the end of the system where a class learned all at the same speed, formal phonetics is no longer viable. Even teaching phonetics in groups falls into the difficulties we have mentioned.

The main complication of phonics is that many of the most commonly used words show the greatest divergences in spelling and pronunciation. It is interesting to speculate on what happens in French for instance, where many word endings are left silent and there are many elisions. Children do not build up long words from single sounds but from syllables or from familiar groupings of letters. For instance the word 'meaningless' might be built up from 'mean-ing-less' but it would never be built up from 'm-ea-n-i-n-g-l-e-ss'.

The fact that phonics is unfashionable has tended to detract from the learning of the alphabet, which is a bad mistake. Apart from the fact that children actually enjoy saying the alphabet and looking at A.B.C. books, the alphabet is a useful basic tool, even in early stages. It is used in dictionaries and indexing. When the alphabet is learned, the names and sounds of the letters should be taught together. I have received varying directions from head teachers and lecturers anxious to be up with the latest fashion, such as 'Don't teach the alphabet, it's out', 'Always use sounds and never letter names', 'Avoid capitals'!! I would advise teachers to be eclectic, keeping much of the old, while evaluating the new, but never being a slave to fashion.

i.t.a.

The Initial Teaching Alphabet represents a *reductio ad absurdum*. The aim is to produce more logical English script by means of extra phonetic characters and augmenting the ordinary alphabet, apart from X and Q, with twenty further characters, representing some diphthongs, i.e. combined vowel sounds, and variants of common consonants. The design is purely arbitrary. There is, for example, no systematic attempt to represent all the phonetic sounds of English or to get rid of redundant symbols (e.g. both C and K have a 'hard' sound). The most glaring omission is any symbol for the neutral vowel of English 'er', what the Oxford dictionary calls indeterminates and which is written 'ə' by phoneticians, for example:

a̲go, pro̲ceed, p̲articular, commo̲n, sacra̲me̲nt, and numero̲us othe̲r insta̲nces in this sentence.

Because it is arbitrary, the Initial Teaching Alphabet cannot solve all the problems of the inconsistencies arising from English spelling. It can solve only some of them, possibly the worst. Therefore it can claim to be only a partial solution of the spelling problem. Nevertheless the scheme has been heavily promoted and a major experiment has been undertaken involving a large number of schools, with the object of justifying it. The trouble with experiments of this kind is the difficulty of preserving a scientific atmosphere. Teachers taking part in the experiment will feel themselves on test and are likely to make more of an effort. The control group should have been put on an equal footing in order to compare the optimum performance of either method, assuming that the control group represented a single method. I have no doubt that many children will learn to read with the help of the Initial Teaching Alphabet, but the same children would have learned to read by other methods. The acid test, one which might well justify the large investment needed to switch to the Initial Teaching Alphabet, would be the performance of those children, who by normal methods would leave school illiterate. In order to measure this convincingly, years of rigorous experimentation would be necessary.

The pamphlet 'i.t.a and your child' claims that 'the alphabet designed by Sir James Pitman is an attempt to help your child start reading on a more logical basis. This means that he does not have to cope with all the irregularities of normal spelling until he is more mature'. This idea seems to confuse 'reading' and 'spelling'.

The examples given in the pamphlet of 'I', 'pie', 'time', 'high', 'my', 'buy', are possibly less confusing to the reader than ie, pie, tiem, hie, mie, bie. A discerning teacher will notice that many children find similar-looking words very difficult to distinguish. Spelling is quite a different matter. Any child who is taught a smattering of phonics will usually spell phonically at first. He will have to learn to spell correctly in the end so there will be no advantage in having learned this temporary spelling of the Initial Teaching Alphabet. In fact most children develop their own version of applied phonic spelling. Children do not learn to read by building up a word from its component parts and it is evident that the authors of i.t.a. recognize this, when they allow for example,

1. <u>mummy</u> (y as in yellow) rather than 'mumi'.
2. <u>first</u> with the ambiguity or 'ir' retained. (Incidentally the variant of the 'back' r is distinguished only by a faint stroke thus 'r' as in red and 'ɾ' as in bird. This must be very difficult for a child to distinguish.)
3. <u>blacken</u> retains a redundant 'k' sound. The price of keeping both 'c' and 'k' as hard sounds is that the more important soft 'c' must be replaced by 's'. On the one hand the i.t.a. people are at pains to point out that 'kitten' is not 'citten', yet they avoid the fact that words like ceiling must begin with 's' which will only add confusion to a younger speller.

Since learning phonics is a very difficult process, (even more difficult than learning whole words) I see no advantage for the slow reader in the Initial Teaching Alphabet and the quick reader is equally at home with the ordinary alphabet. Once again we are back to the situation where the same children are as good at one technique as another and the children who find it difficult to grasp whole words are no more able to grasp the analytical approach.

The authors of the i.t.a. scheme claim that the child is ready to make the transition to reading our ordinary alphabet when he can 'read fluently'. Fluently at what level? we are entitled to ask. Every teacher knows that fluency at one grade of reader does not necessarily extend to the next, but the parent is assured 'the teacher will know'. The game is given away by the explanation 'By the time a child is ready for the transition, <u>he should be reading for the meaning</u> of the story and so the sounding of each

27

word letter by letter, syllable by syllable does not occur.' (The emphasis is mine.) What on earth have they been reading for all this time? This sums up the failure of all reading methods. They are products of a mechanistic outlook.

The Initial Teaching Alphabet in attempting to solve one problem has created another, which is of course the transition from the artificial language to the real alphabet. This must be very painful for a child who is transferred to a non i.t.a. school, but all i.t.a. pupils have to face it eventually. Is it not likely that the less able children will find the greatest confusion in learning a further set of rules and be prone to give up the unequal struggle? Supposing i.t.a. represented a real achievement, we should have to measure the cost. The cost turns out to be high. First there is the physical cost of producing the material. Because there will be a large overlap between i.t.a. books and ordinary books, as children make the transition at different levels, there will have to be investment by schools, libraries, and book shops to keep sufficient stocks in both languages. In any case, as long as i.t.a. is experimental some children will be deprived of the variety of exciting books written in our funny old alphabet. One can also imagine the confusion if small children choose the wrong book in the library or are given the wrong book by an uninformed aunt. This is a further inhibition on the slow reader. If a child is not ready to make the transition till he is ten plus, is he to be denied all literature, except that available from i.t.a. publishers? The alternative is the duplication of every child's book, the cost of which will be phenomenal. We hear a good deal about deprived children. Would this not be a severe and subtle deprivation? Thus there is a cost over and above the physical cost which would be difficult to measure. The child is going to be cut off for an undefined period from all the written messages in his environment. For words are not confined to books just as books are not confined to schools. The learner reader delights in recognizing words in signs, labels, newspapers, comics, TV captions, shop windows, and so on. We must conclude that the price is not worth paying.

Reading through interest – the first consumer approach to teaching reading

The greatest single influence on modern reading has been Nora L. Goddard's. Her book 'Reading in the Modern Infants' School' has probably had more to do with the look of a modern classroom and the organization of its reading activities than any other influence. This came about not through the invention of a new method but through the recognition of the part played by interest in the child's approach to reading. This is in effect the first 'consumer approach' to reading which like many such approaches seems obvious once it has been made, but must have required great imagination and forcefulness to get accepted. Like many pioneers Miss Goddard has not wholly thrown off her links with past attitudes. She can at the same time as recommending an 'approach through interest, which is so important throughout the child's life in infant school' ask for a balance to be struck with 'the more formal and systematic side of the work'. By keeping this separation she has had little influence on the reading books, which count as the formal and systematic side, but she has helped to integrate reading with other classroom activities. Modern teachers now have a lot of scope to create their own reading material to use as labels and captions in play and on the classroom walls. Unfortunately reading-through-interest falls down if this is all there is to it, and the reading books themselves are not interesting. Although Miss Goddard has drawn up careful criteria for the evaluation of reading schemes and other literature in her book these are completely abstract and un-critical, no individual reading scheme is mentioned, and most surprisingly, interest is not mentioned as a criterion. Thus reading-through-interest has come to be applied to essentially non-reading activities, i.e. where the reading is secondary to what is going on. Valuable as they are, reading-through-interest techniques, such as labelling children's models and pictures, signposting play activities, and writing news books, are some-what limited in scope. I feel that there is a danger that they may become ritualized, making too many demands on the teacher's

29

time and effort and not necessarily reflecting the interest of every child.

Reading through writing?

Writing does assist reading but the process works more effectively in reverse. A child cannot write well until he can read well. Occasionally one finds a child who is more interested in learning to write than in learning to read, and obviously here the writing helps the reading. In general, however, writing ability depends on a modicum of reading ability. Where writing can assist reading is in the additions to vocabulary that come from the children's request for spellings.

Many teachers give the child a little home-made dictionary with the main purpose of helping in writing. These dictionaries consist of a little exercise book with each page labelled with a letter of the alphabet. When the child has a spelling query he first of all has to find the appropriate page in his dictionary so that the teacher can write in the correct spelling. These word-books help a child to learn the alphabet, words, and their sounds. It is surprising that these books do not appear to be available for schools in a printed form, e.g. with a visible letter index, like a personal telephone directory. It would be important to show all the various forms a letter can take, for example G g 9. Children often have difficulty in finding letters in alphabetical order and a visible index would overcome this. When the alphabetical principle has been established a child can pass on to a picture dictionary. These consist of words accompanied by relevant illustrations. It goes without saying that many words cannot be illustrated. Other words need some explanation which involves using a sentence with the appropriate word underlined. This restricts the use of a picture dictionary to quite advanced readers. The frustration of not finding familiar abstract words also reduces their value. Beyond a certain stage however, a picture dictionary helps children to find out for themselves and relieves the pressure on the teacher to provide spellings.

Breakthrough to literacy

A new reading programme with the impressive title of 'Breakthrough to Literacy' has just been put on the market to the accompaniment of a great deal of publicity. It needs to be evaluated here, not so much for its content, but upon its claims as an entirely new technique. 'Breakthrough to Literacy' lays the stress upon the arrangement of words. It depends principally upon the child constructing his own sentences or phrases with a kit called a Sentence Maker. This consists of a folder containing words printed on small pieces of plastic. The child can slot the words into a stand in order to make sentences. In addition to words chosen by the publisher there are blank pieces which the teacher may fill in with the child's own choice of words. This new system is said to be based upon extensive research. It is completely new and therefore difficult to pronounce upon. However, the first problem that must arise is that of keeping the bits together, and making sure they are not swept up by the cleaner overnight! Undeniably it seems a cumbersome idea to have these permanent words. Supposing a word does find its way to the floor, one can imagine the problems of sorting out whose word it is. Apart from this clumsy aspect of the scheme the main weakness is that it depends upon 'writing' being put before 'reading'. Certainly the child is not wielding a pencil or coping with spelling, but he still has to select and phrase his words. He must need an ever-increasing pool of plastic words or be faced with a need to restrict his text. One wonders therefore in what way this new scheme is an improvement on good old-fashioned paper and pencil. These remain considerably more flexible and since a child has to learn at some stage how to form his letters he might as well do this from the start. Since I feel very strongly that writing must follow reading, I see no advantage to this method and indeed I am inclined to find it retrogressive. Even if I were to be proved wrong I still envisage a lot of trouble in supervising it. I feel 'Breakthrough to Literacy' will suffer the fate of other bitty devices such as Colour Factor and Cuisinère rods in mathematics. The teacher may well give up trying to

31

keep the many small pieces together and will be forgiven for discreetly tucking them away at the back of the cupboard. At first sight the reading material accompanying this programme looks more attractive than most early material, but not having been able to use it with my children, I cannot evaluate it fairly.

The Language Master

Another new product which is attracting attention at the moment is a machine called the Language Master. This is a sort of tape recorder into which flash cards can be slotted. The top of the card shows a word. The bottom of the card consists of a dual track magnetic tape strip. When the card is slotted in, one of the tracks can be controlled by the teacher, and the other by the child. Thus the teacher can record the word on the card and the child can record the word on his part of the tape. Alternatively either can record a sentence about the word, or in fact anything they like. By removing a small key the teacher can prevent her track being erased or interfered with by the child. One is forced to the conclusion that the Language Master is an expensive novelty which has little original purpose, and which will pall just as quickly on the children as conventional flash cards do in any case. Its drawback as a self teaching device is that it is incapable of response, except that of direct playback, and of course it is unable to represent any emotion or reward. The incentive for success in flash card work is the teacher's pleasure and delight. If devices of this sort can help backward readers, or remedial groups, in any way whatsoever, then their price will be justified but in a normal classroom situation their very limited usefulness must be weighed against the equivalent cost of extra books.

The desire to catch up

Two important but neglected factors in learning to read are the child's own sense of achievement and the need for the teacher's constant encouragement. Like any other learner a child must feel he is getting on. It is undeniable that some snobbery exists in the classroom, according to children's reading ability.

Teachers and publishers have reacted against this by substituting titles for numbers on reading books. Children are not fooled and are fully aware of the sequence of the titles. The real difficulty lies in the thickness and the spacing of the books. It is far better to have a large series of quickly-read thin books than one or two thick ones. Finishing a book in itself gives a child a great sense of achievement. The greater number of books he finishes the greater will be his morale. Some publishers have designed series of about six books to span three years. It is unthinkable that a child should be condemned to spend more than a few weeks on a book. After a certain period the usefulness of a book must be subject to diminishing returns. In other words although the book may continue to have some value it has less value than a fresh book. It would be useful if the publishers could be persuaded to consider these problems.

The snobbery we mention is really quite harmless and can be put to good use by the teacher. One way is for the advanced readers to help the slower ones, by telling them words, hearing them read, or reading to them. The bright readers can easily be prevented from getting arrogant, by playing up the weaker readers' other accomplishments. The other way is to control the spirit of competition that exists among small children. The desire to catch up is very strong. Many children respond to personal records, such as cards recording books completed. A further incentive is a series of books separate from the class library and the reading scheme, to be read through by the child on his own in the way of a reward for progress. Some children like these special books to be recorded, as the feeling of getting on is as important as the pleasure of reading. Some aspects of teaching children to read are extremely tedious. Incessant demands to be heard, and the endless repetition of the same trite phrases, impress on any sensitive teacher the need for more varied and interesting material. Yet it is vitally necessary to hear children read at every stage and always to appear excited and thrilled at the progress made. Equally it is quite wrong to be cross or disappointed if no apparent progress has been made. The normal age of learning to read coincides with tremendous emotional dependence on the teacher and a number of children clearly learn to read just to please the teacher.

Although we have mentioned how useful it is for the better readers to help the slower ones, we do not advocate any formal arrangements such as reading partners, as this can be a burden on children. But in an informal atmosphere children help each other spontaneously. With today's classes of forty children it is physically impossible to allocate more than a few minutes per week to hearing each child read. Nonetheless every extra minute is precious and produces noticeable results.

Books of familiar nursery rhymes, poems, and songs are a great asset to reading. They are usually popular and because they are known in advance they can be read with ease and strange words can be absorbed without any trouble. Slow readers are especially helped in this way as they get a great sense of achievement from apparently being able to sail through a difficult piece.

All successful techniques for teaching children to read are basically devices to encourage a child to read as much as possible himself and any artifice which persuades a child to read and carry on reading will succeed. The art of teaching, like the art of acting, should be in the background and several of the formal techniques we have described interfere with the teacher's natural talent and aptitude.

3 Current reading schemes

Drawing up criteria

   The teacher can fully evaluate a scheme only by using it and observing the children's and her own reactions to it.

My own experience extends to most published reading schemes. They break down into two groups. The first consists of four leading schemes, which I have used extensively. The second group is made up of undistinguished and indistinguishable competitors, which do not appear worth switching to, though they may provide some supplementary material.

At this point it is important to state by what criteria these schemes must be assessed. It would be wrong to think entirely in terms of a scheme either succeeding or failing in teaching children to read. Bad schemes are preserved because 'they work'. In this sense all schemes succeed and only children or teachers fail. What we should be asking is how efficient a scheme is both in the short term and in the long term. We must enquire how many, and which, children learn to read and at what speed. We must consider how much interest is being stimulated and how much ground work is being laid for further reading. We must ask what the scheme costs in respect of the children's and the teacher's time.

A lot of this has simply to do with how interesting or how boring a scheme is. No matter how scientifically planned a scheme is, if it bores the children and the teacher it is a poor scheme. When a child is bored by a scheme book he reads only the minimum. This may satisfy his teacher but the child's true progress has been slowed down. If a book is interesting and the child carries on reading of his own accord his reading will improve by leaps and bounds.

This elementary point seems to have been obscured by the didactic approach to reading and perhaps the still widely held belief that learning should be slightly unpleasant in order to have its full effect.

When we come to draw up a list of criteria, the factor which will be overwhelmingly important, will be the popularity with the children of the set of books in the scheme. This can be judged only from experience with different sets of children. Books that teachers like do not necessarily go over with the children. An attractive appearance can sometimes conceal an uninteresting text. Books that are considered to have a high literary or moral value may get no response from children. We may help fluent readers to choose what *we* consider to be good books but during the earlier stages of learning we should lean completely towards the children's preferences.

What makes a book a winner?

If we try and put ourselves in the children's place it is possible to see what, from our observations, are the things that make a book a winner. I cannot stress enough the importance of an exciting vocabulary. It used to come as a surprise to teachers of reading to find that children could remember a big word like 'aeroplane' more easily than a small word like 'this'. This did not mean that children could more easily remember big words; they would not have remembered 'individual' or 'information' or 'integrate'. The word 'aeroplane' is an exciting word because it represents an exciting idea. Words like aeroplane, spacemen, rocket launcher, explode, bomb, ghost, kill – these are highly-charged 'evocative' words. Words of this kind tend to be associated more with boys' interests, but boys in general have the most difficulty in learning to read. (A boy of my acquaintance who was a slow reader in his seventh year could read and write only one word, 'Mummy'. To my surprise I found it was the Egyptian bandaged type and not the domestic kind.) Girls have less need of excitement but the same principles hold. Words which are often described as 'key' words such as this, the, they, is, says, can, etc. because they are extremely common linking words, in themselves are uninteresting. They are particularly boring when their repetition is forced on the reader. They will in any case have a high natural repetition. A reading text should be built around interesting, evocative words and not these utility words, which should be subordinate.]

The teacher-orientation is obvious in the average reading text which is crammed with instructions and commands, e.g. look, see, come, go, here is, there is, this is, that is. These consciously and unconsciously emphasize spatial relationships and definitions, ignoring the psychology of a young child. Children of this age are extremely subjective and not interested in definitions and spatial relationships. They are both inquisitive and acquisitive but above all they have a strong sense of excitement and wonder at the world.

An illustration of our argument is what happens to the word 'here' in the 'Janet and John' series. It is an essential word in the first book, 'Here we go', but as the series progresses, its frequency of use decreases sharply and for many children it once again becomes an unfamiliar word when they meet it in later texts. The whole point of repetition is to enable the child to learn a word. There seems no advantage in giving this dull word special treatment at a very early stage if the meaningful repetition cannot be maintained and children have in effect to relearn it in context.

The scope for good stories

Another basic requirement is for the material to tell a story. Most early readers are purely descriptive. Undoubtedly the problems of telling a story with a limited vocabulary are great but more skilful use could be made of illustration. Most readers have pictures which attempt to illustrate the text (with difficulties which we shall discuss later). A better approach might be for the pictures to tell the story, with words as comment or subtitles. One otherwise indifferent reading scheme starts inspiringly with a one word story 'Splash'. This story illustrates a technique which could perhaps be developed.

What are the qualities which go to make a good story? The successful ingredients are adventure and humour.

Early readers tend to rely on creating interest in the child by showing identifiable characters in identifiable situations. But nowhere is the scene of domestic bliss disrupted by someone breaking a cup or spilling the milk. Our little heroes and heroines are always polite, helpful, or playing nicely, in fact little prigs. Yet the success of Dorothy Edward's 'My Naughty Little Sister' series and Leila Berg's 'Little Pete', as stories for reading to children, depend on adding naughtiness and mischief to identification. My Naughty Little Sister stories also give the children a delicious feeling of superiority.

As a child progresses through a reading series, and his reading vocabulary is enlarged, the scope for good stories is increased. The most generally popular are the traditional tales. Their popularity is enhanced by familiarity. On the one hand this is comforting, children preferring to read and reread old favourites at this age, and on the other hand there is a sense of achievement from being able to read the same stories as the teacher reads. It is argued that one cannot assess a child's comprehension, or even be sure that he has actually read a story, if the material is already familiar. However I feel that if a child can read a randomly selected paragraph well enough to satisfy the teacher this is an adequate test of ability.

I have asked a class of late six-year-olds, containing thirty good readers, which school reading book they liked best. A few chose their current reading book, a few chose their very first reading book, but the overwhelming vote went to Beacons books 3, 4, and 5, 'The Pancake', 'Careful Hans', and 'Briar Rose'. Yet most of them had read many different reading series. I am not advocating the use of traditional tales exclusively but there seem to be few good modern equivalents.

Maintaining interest with a small vocabulary

Two further factors which influence the popularity of a reader with children, are the span of attention required and the sense of achievement when the book is finished. Since children are not able to concentrate for long, and need as many fillips as they can get, the ideal is a short but reasonably impressive book. Most reading schemes, no doubt for reasons of economy, are in over-large volumes. For example, the Beacons mentioned above run to approximately seventy pages of closely-packed text. The younger the child the less he can cope. Therefore the system is in serious need of review by educational publishers. Five-year-olds who are able to read Beacons 3 and 4 become frustrated and bogged down because they cannot recognize their own progress and achievement. Suitable graded material for five-year-olds who can read is extremely scarce. (Here I am not thinking of the above-average five-year-old who can dispense with a reading scheme altogether.) The problem is not confined to the Beacons. Five-year-olds who can read, suffer severely from the defects of all reading schemes. Possibly some of these defects may be overcome by better and simpler presentation, along the lines I have suggested, of material originally conceived for an older age group.

Other aspects that can interfere with enjoyment, that we have already touched upon, are badly told stories, the portrayal of anachronistic environments, poor design and layout, and poor physical condition of a book.

It is difficult to lay down any rules about design and layout as this is an area where rules should be broken. However, in general, clarity and simplicity will be best, making for a small amount of text on each page or spread, with plenty of easily understandable pictures and intelligent use of colour. At the same time it would be disastrous to encourage a bland formula. Novelty and variety and a sense of pace are just as much to be encouraged.

An attractively inviting permanent cover is another valuable feature which is often surprisingly botched by educational publishers who nevertheless have many outstanding examples to learn from in the book shops. Similarly a book which is tattered and dirty can hardly be expected to inspire a child.

All the factors that I have mentioned represent means of making as attractive as possible a small starting vocabulary and of maintaining interest after the first steps have been taken.

A good reading scheme should have a small starting vocabulary and a very gradual introduction of new words. It will give the children a sense of achievement and prevent them from being overwhelmed by new words. It must cater for the quite different speeds at which children learn. This can best be done by providing a great deal more supplementary material for the slower readers. In this way they can keep the momentum and at the same time avoid the feeling of failure from having to repeat a book. The shortage of such material arises partly because the need is not recognized and partly because of a lack of ingenuity in designing variations within a limited vocabulary. A child need not know every single word in a book before he passes on to the next.

Again the lack of opportunity to move sideways leads to a hesitant reader being punished by being forced into rote learning. Some teachers, from misplaced thoroughness, not only expect the child to know every word in the book, they even expect him to read the glossary before he moves on. A glossary is simply an aid for the teacher and in spite of the efforts of publishers to make it clear that it is not for the children's use, this dreadful practice is still carried on. It is astonishing that a child who has read a book fluently but may fail to recognize words in a glossary is made brutally aware that he has not in fact 'read' the book because he does not know the words. The fact that words put in this form can appear meaningless even to intelligent children does not occur to some teachers. This is quite simply a sterile approach because it demands all-or-nothing recognition of words. The teacher need not fear that the child will not be able to read the next book because once the words are allowed to come to life in an attractive and meaningful context they will have a better chance of passing into his reading vocabulary and staying there. What is more, word-use will be enhanced as distinct from word-recognition.

Supplementary reading material should in no circumstances be inferior to basic reading material, especially as it is most used by slower readers in order to slow down the rate of introduction of new words and give increased repetition.

The ideal reading scheme will balance adequate repetition, the need to maintain interest, and the phased introduction of new words. These requirements may seem simple but it can be safely stated that they are never met. The almost intractable problems are firstly that repetition of words is an extremely complex matter; secondly that interest varies with age and cultural considerations, thirdly that the introduction of new words is bound to be an arbitrary affair. Let us concentrate for the moment on the problems of repetition, relating it to interest and new vocabulary.

The trap of the key words concept

Reading schemes fail because, whether or not they try to be scientific, repetition is achieved at the price of monotony, ambiguity, banality, and too often absurdity. It is the schemes which have tried hardest to be scientific which tend to fall into these traps, and which by minimizing context show a lack of concern for meaning, and a failure to appreciate that language is more than the sum of its parts.

The parts that get the most emphasis are those described or understood as 'key' words. The logic behind this concept would run as follows: 'There are some words in the language that are used much more than others, it is obvious then that these *must* be learned first'. This kind of thinking ignores the nature of these frequently used words and overlooks the fact that they have a high natural repetition. These words tend to be by their nature, utilitarian linking words. Too forced a repetition within a limited context is almost bound to be boring. What is more they resist illustration, they lack emotional appeal, and they are often difficult to distinguish, e.g. the, them, then, they, there, their, this, that. It is easy to demonstrate that information and emotion are carried by non-key words. I have taken a passage entirely at random from a child's book, 'James and the Giant Peach' by Roald Dahl, page 44. I have separated the words used into two groups. The first comprises words appearing among the sixty-eight which, according to the Ladybird scheme, make up half of those in common use. The second group is the remainder.

Group 1

And now the ..... had ..... out of the ..... and was over the ..... of the ..... and ..... down the ..... at a ..... and ..... and ..... it went, and the ..... of ..... who were ..... up the ..... of this ..... down ..... them and they ..... and ..... to right and ..... as it went ..... by.

Group 2

peach ..... broken ..... garden ..... edge ..... hill, rolling ..... bouncing ..... steep slope ..... terrific pace. Faster ..... faster ..... faster ..... crowds ..... people ..... climbing ..... hill suddenly caught sight ..... terrible monster plunging ..... upon ..... screamed ..... scattered ..... left ..... hurtling.

Obviously the first passage has no particular meaning. It expresses relationships, but leaves the reader completely in the dark as to what objects are related and in what manner. The second passage vividly describes a scene and the omission of the useful words actually becomes a stylistic device. An excited account concentrates on the important words, which carry a lot of information and leaves out merely connecting words.

In this connection Charles Dickens' character, Mr Jingle, springs to mind. He was able to make a great deal of sense with the minimum use of 'key' words. 'Kent Sir – everybody knows Kent – apples, cherries, hops and women'. (Pickwick Papers).

The case of Mr Jingle draws attention to the fact that when we want to convey information we draw on the 19,900 other words which make up the other half of common word frequency according to the authors of the 'Ladybird Key Words Reading Scheme'.

Their central tenet is, that 'children learn to read more easily and quickly if the first words they learn are the most used words in the language'. Even if a child is taught to recognize perfectly the sixty-eight words that make up half the language, he still is nowhere near being able to read and he has probably been given the wrong model of the language. He still has the hard slog of learning the other 19,900 words. This seems impossible and that is why a key word scheme, which concentrates on an apparently logical selection appears so attractive. But from the standpoint of the language as a whole, any small selection of words is going to be arbitrary unless it reflects all the different kinds of words in the language, and the way they are put together. What we are however entitled to say from the evidence about the frequency of distribution of words is 'How fortunate we are that certain words crop up very frequently in reading and get a large amount of natural repetition. Let us concentrate on finding among less used words an interesting vocabulary on which to build the whole art of reading'.

The need for a more balanced initial vocabulary

We have already touched on criteria for selecting this model vocabulary but of course they will involve looking at words to see how well they relate to the child's world and imagination. Start with this two-tier structure of 'potent' words and naturally frequent words, bring in a concern for phrasing and we should soon see better results from the effort and ingenuity that now goes into arranging early reading from the thin material of key words.

Children who are able to read early are usually enthusiastic enough to be unaffected by the drawbacks of forced repetition. But the majority of children are affected by forced repetition and stilted phrasing. Whatever their intelligence they find it ulti-

43

mately discouraging. The slower the reading progress and the older the child the more attention has to be paid to designing texts with repetition which insults neither the intelligence nor the status of the child. The flexible approach we advocate has the merit of not insisting on the repetition of the same few dull words.

A more balanced initial vocabulary would allow more appropriate illustration than is encountered in most schemes. In the earliest readers the pictures should give the clue to the text. Frequently they are quite unrelated and a bright child will read what ought to be written there and not what actually is. All reading schemes are reluctant to introduce too many concrete nouns either for reasons of general economy or because they are much less common than connecting words. This is a pity because it is easier to illustrate objects than concepts or relationships, and if nouns can be supported by pictures more of them can be afforded.

The Ladybird Key Words Reading Scheme

The Ladybird scheme has borne the brunt of our criticism so far. This is because it is highly favoured at the moment and because it is one of the most up-to-date schemes. We now ought to give an assessment of Ladybirds which includes well-deserved favourable comments as well as the criticisms already mentioned to illustrate various points.

The Ladybird Key Words scheme starts well enough and is indeed appealing to beginning readers. The illustrations are bright and up-to-date. The type is large and clear. The picture: text ratio is good and of course the vocabulary is small, sixteen words initially. The content is insipid but the joy of beginning is enough to carry children through the first three books. For the average child the gradient between the books is not too extreme. It is interesting to inquire at this point how, and indeed why, certain reading ages are assigned to each Ladybird stage. Thus books 1a, 1b, and 1c are given a reading age of four to four and a half years. 2a, 2b, and 2c, four and a half to five years and so on at six-monthly intervals up to 12a, 12b, and 12c, for nine and a half to ten years. Several questions arise. Are these average or

44

optimum reading ages? Does the programme of reading represent exclusive concentration on Ladybird? If it does not, at what point does the reading capacity branch out? Otherwise do children of nine and a half read only Ladybirds? Does the extreme symmetry of the scheme, whereby three books occupy each half year for six years, have any relationship to reality? . . . . The publishers claim that 'reading fluency will have been achieved when the learner has worked through all the thirty-six books'. It appears also that he will have a vocabulary of 1,934 words. No doubt this claim is based on commercial reasoning but it does represent a sausage machine attitude to reading and what is more the removal of any responsibility for failure from the publishers. After a brisk start, at least for the majority of children, the series becomes monotonous and plodding. At Book Four the children lose their spontaneous desire to read, and when reading starts to become hard work, Ladybird Book Four makes sure that it is. The signs are complete loss of concentration and excessive wriggling while reading. The gentle virtues of the first books have become liabilities when carried through to later books, where more excitement, variety, and cultural breadth are needed.

Here is page 12 from Book 5a, quoted in full to give an example of the banality of the text.

They all go in. 'Here you are,' says the man, 'here is some milk for you.' Jane and Peter and Mummy have some of the milk, and Daddy says, 'Now I want some, please.'

The man works on the farm and he likes to talk to them about it. He talks about the cows, and he talks about the pigs. He likes his work.

Then Daddy talks to the man about the walk. He says where they want to go. 'Yes' says the man, 'I like to walk up the hill. I like to be up there. You can see the sea.'

He gives Pat some milk.

There is no continuity; the next page starts with an abrupt transition to the top of a hill, viz:

They can see the top now. They can see the top of the hill.

We have already suggested that all the various reading schemes 'work' with the majority of children and with an enthusiastic teacher. The residual problem of children who fail to read is shrugged off. Not surprisingly, the Ladybird scheme fails to make any impact on this sizeable minority (varying of course with district and age group) who find difficulty in starting to read. This group of children remains completely uninterested in whether 'Peter is here' or 'Jane is here' etc. This goes not only for less bright children but also for a group of bright children who make imaginative guesses at the text on the basis of the illustrations. For example a picture of Jane skipping is captioned 'I like Jane' or a picture of Peder playing with a boat is captioned 'I like Peter'. What is one to make of the intelligent child who reads this as 'Jane is skipping' or 'Peter's got a boat'. The teacher has the problem of diverting the child from its perfectly logical position by insisting that 'that is not what it says'. In short such a book either strikes no spark or strikes the wrong sparks.

Now that schemes like 'Ladybird' present themselves in a scientific manner to basically unscientific people it is difficult to determine how the publishers see their scheme developing. Teachers are not in a position to question the scientific basis of such things as the Key word distribution. My study of it suggests that it is to some extent self-confirming in the sense that its source material is exactly the type of book which represents conventional reading material for children. It is rather disconcerting for example to find that among the 150 most-used words in English are 'rabbit', 'pig', 'jam', 'farm', 'cow', and 'apple'.

The verdict on Ladybird is that the early books are mildly attractive but the narrowness and smugness of the text become stifling at a very early point in the series. The scientific justification of the key word scheme, while seeming plausible, is somewhat dubious.

The Janet and John Series

'Janet and John' is still a widely used scheme and must represent the most profitable return on a few colour plates in the history of publishing. A series of twee ill-drawn illustrations shows Janet and John in scenes from suburban life circa 1930. It is impertinent of the publishers to foist the same dreary pictures on children and teachers for decade after decade and to allow such a narrow and sentimental view of life. A curiosity about Janet and John is the way they stand and move and react to things. Anyone used to children would see that they are physiological and psychological three-year-olds! This is nothing less than insulting to children of seven. The total effect of the pictures, even before we consider the words, is a complete separation from life. Even if we accept its conventions the little world of Janet and John provides insipid and monotonous fare. The texts are downright silly and an affront to even the dimmest child. The fact of their continued use in schools is surprising, except that one has to admit they represent the best of a very bad lot. The Janet and John series achieves my reluctant accolade chiefly as a result of its supplementary material, which is arranged in small books more easily assimilated by young readers. This makes children aware of their own progress, which appears more rapid the smaller the books are. The most successful of the supplementary books are the ones based on traditional stories, in spite of unnecessarily archaic constructions, e.g. 'Mr Vinegar started home'. This no doubt arises from the somewhat dubious demands of 'vocabulary control'.

Like 'Ladybirds' the Janet and John system has been based on the notion of word frequency rather than on any considerations of syntax or colloquialism or even meaning. Apart from the irritation caused by a simple and useful idea being built up into a pseudo-science, one feels suspicion of the validity of the approach.

47

As I have mentioned before, an uncritical acceptance of reported word frequencies can lead to their uncritical application. The fallacy is that ostensibly in order to take advantage of the high natural frequency of certain words, completely artificial and distorted texts are produced to force this frequency. It would seem logical that any text would be made easier by the natural repetition of 'key words'. If these key words do not occur often enough in this way there seems little point in making intensive use of them.

Janet and John suffer from severe distortion to fit in certain words at high frequency. It leads to gibberish of the following kind taken from 'Out and About' pages 6 and 7.

> 'This is Janet's home
> This is John's home
> It is a green house
> Look at the green house
> Father is in it
> It is Father's home too'.

Apart from the sheer dullness of it, here are some of the misinterpretations read into it, bearing in mind these statements are accompanied by a picture of three houses of various unlikely colours. Janet and John can be credited with a house each. Daddy can be credited with a second house. They can all be credited with living in a green house. Having been told to look at the green house because Father is in it, one's fears about what sinister motive he may have there are allayed by being told it is 'home'. One little boy I knew found it all very funny. When asked why he was laughing, he replied 'because Father has two homes'. The phrasing is un-English and the repetition is negated by ambiguity. This ... This ... is used in English to introduce two separate things. The obsession with words means that the important possessive Janet's and John's is slipped in casually. The word 'it' is used merely as a clumsy link word. One can work out how these sentences could be rephrased while remaining simple.

'Janet and John live in a green house. You can see it here. Look, Father is at home etc.'

The important point is that dealing with 'house' and 'home' calls out for the introduction of the word 'live'. 'Home' could be introduced in the context of being 'at home', 'coming home', before the introduction of the singular possessive. Children insist 'This is Janet's house'. They also say 'this is my house' or 'where I live' but 'I am going home'. (It is striking to notice that two books after the introduction of the awful pair the word 'their' is not available.)

It is a grave error to simplify so much that our language becomes incorrect because any reasonably intelligent child will read what *ought* to be there.

Just how sacrosanct the brick-by-brick approach is, and with what horror the intuitive approach is held, can be seen from the following quotation taken from the Janet and John Manual, page 45:

'Those who will not teach phonics for fear that the child, using a logical approach should sometimes get an unsatisfactory result, are often quite content for him to get an equally unsatisfactory result from an illogical process like guessing from context'.

If the context made sense the *guess* would more than likely be an accurate one. In an illogical context like 'Janet and John' children will have difficulty even with familiar words. Guessing is based on probability, and an unnatural language lacking the hints and clues given by normal speech patterns will lead to low probabilities, i.e. bad guesses.

The Janet and John system includes the option of a so-called 'whole word course' and slightly apologetically a 'phonic course'. The material for each is virtually identical and the same strictures apply.

From the point of view of satisfying the children and giving them a sense of achievement, the main Janet and John readers are too bulky and too heavy-going, although as I mentioned, the supplementary readers are good in this respect. The 'Extension Readers' appear somewhat superfluous as they carry a reading system beyond the point where children should have free choice of reading, and certainly should have left 'Janet and John' behind.

All in all the Janet and John system is banal, self-satisfied, and basically unscientific.

The Beacon Readers

The Beacon series is another well-established system which through being less 'scientific' has fallen somewhat out of favour. This is a pity because after a disastrous start the Beacon series contains some useful and attractive material. The early books, in spite of superficial modernization, i.e. different covers and illustrations, are quite unsuitable for beginning reading for most children. The faults of the Beacons are firstly a starting vocabulary which is too large and too steep; secondly a text which is mawkish and at times inscrutable (for instance the 'cum-je-cum' game); thirdly the books are too thick and there is no supplementary material to accompany the first readers. What used to be Beacons numbers 3, 4, and 5, now renamed The Pancake, Careful Hans, and Briar Rose respectively, are full of good well-presented traditional tales and are very popular with children. The books, though, are still far too thick. There is some supplementary material, also of quite good quality.

The Happy Venture Series

The Happy Venture series combines the faults of all the reading series we have mentioned without any mitigating virtues. The books are too large, the text is invariably banal and archaic. The illustrations, even after modernization, are unbelievably bad and still out-of-date. The layout is unattractive. The redesigned covers are still completely without interest. Children exposed to Happy Ventures quickly lose their interest and enthusiasm for reading. Happy Ventures is yet another system based on a 'scientific' theory of language. Its failure must demonstrate that this theory does not go deeply enough or that the theory has been poorly applied. The author of the scheme provides a wider and more sympathetic base than merely a word-incidence approach. However, the drawback of all the would-be scientific approaches is that in concentrating on the activity of learning words they lose sight of the language as a whole.

There are a number of other established reading schemes with varying degrees of pretension. I will not provide a critique of these schemes since on detailed examination, the material has looked too off-putting to use the children as guinea pigs. For a lot of teachers the decision not to use a scheme which is being promoted takes a certain amount of nerve, especially if it is in the face of a lot of impressive jargon.

New reading schemes

There are two new schemes worth mentioning. One is 'Through the Rainbow'. The fault here seems to be that in leaning over backwards to be realistic the series succeeds in being merely ordinary. The subject matter dealing with the minutiae of a suburban family is as unexciting as one would expect. The publishers claim that 'it uses the sort of language that children really talk'. The language is as stilted as any other reader, lacking the rhythm and economy of real speech. This is a typical exhausting page from Orange Book 3:

> Is there a playhouse
> in your school
> do you play in the playhouse
> do you have tea
> in the playhouse
> do you have a tea party
> draw yourself having tea
>
> write
> this is me having tea
> in the play house

It is claimed to be 'complete in itself and does not require numbers of supplementary readers at each stage'. Such a claim must rest on children having uniform ability. The use of supplementaries is designed to help slower readers and it is disturbing to find this not recognized. In the early books the scheme dispenses entirely with punctuation, presumably for the sake of simplicity. Children who are ready to read, find no difficulty with capitals and punctuation, and like many other aspects of reading these things fall into place naturally. I was taught a lesson by a reception class when I avoided explaining the presence of a question mark on a wall story. One of the children pointed out the question mark and after that the whole class was very excited at finding question marks in reading texts, though they probably did not comprehend their meaning and certainly many of the children could not read.

The promotion material and the handbook of the Methuen reading series show a perceptive and sympathetic understanding of the problem of teaching reading. One of the central precepts is reading-for-meaning. The editor of the series eschews dogma and does not rely on a narrowly scientific approach. The original inspiration for the series was the actual experience of teachers who contributed ideas and material. Unfortunately it does not live up to its promise. Certainly children do not find the caption books exciting, at least when they have the choice of better children's literature. The larger readers that follow have the usual faults of being too thick, having too much text per page and too few illustrations, and most of the stories are sadly long-winded and banal. The harsh truth may be that writing is a creative act and that however well the analysis has been done and the groundwork laid, literary and artistic talent of a high order must be applied to the finished article. As we have said before, once a frame of reference has been provided there should be no rules. My disappointment raises the question whether, when the right thinking has been done, the publishers are prepared after their initial outlay to spend more money on testing and improvements. There are few signs that publishers or educational authorities are prepared to carry out consumer research on teachers and children – who are the real consumers, which might show the size and commercial value of the opportunity that exists.

An example of the right approach

We should finally mention an outstanding writer who has contributed various series, principally designed for older or junior readers. This is S. K. McCullagh who has produced 'The Griffin Readers', 'The Dragon Books', and the '1 2 3 and Away' series. Some of these books can be used with advantage in infant school, but generally they are too steeply graded for average-to-backward readers. They are a model of the right approach. They are thin books. They have a built-in incentive to carry on to the next volume. The repetition is not artificial but part of the story. The subject matter and the illustrations are exciting or amusing. They neither strain nor insult the readers' intelligence. It is a pity that this author has not applied her skill to a starting series for very young readers.

We have seen that most reading schemes are worthless and where they have a methodology it is frequently suspect. They are strikingly indifferent to what reading attainment actually is, or what it can lead to. As a result they are not in a position to show their validity. It can be fairly argued that children learn to read in spite of reading schemes. It is a stark fact however that many children never learn to read, notwithstanding the earnest efforts of teachers to apply reading schemes. I have the uncomfortable feeling that many children who have learned to read imperfectly will never develop their reading beyond a simple mechanical skill. It is impossible to speculate on the actual harm that may be done by deadening children's appreciation of literature and language.

4 Classroom experience

Reading as part of communal activity
A visitor to a modern infants classroom, especially one of the very informal kind, might be forgiven for being bewildered. There is a great deal going on and a great deal to see. In my classroom for example, we have a library area, a mathematics area, a science table, pet animals, a sand tray, a water tray, a Wendy house, and dressing-up clothes. We have a music corner, and a writing area where pencils, writing books, and dictionaries are kept. There is a creative area where paints, clay, glue, junk materials are used. We have woodwork and bricks, games and toys. Around the room there are pictures, displays of books, models, and exhibitions. The children move about, not always sticking to the ordained areas. Indeed a great deal of flexibility is encouraged. For example scientific experiments may be carried out in the water tray, writing may be done on the floor, but equally there are rules to prevent disorder, such as not taking paints into the library area or doing woodwork in the Wendy house. But the picture of random activity, possibly even of chaos to the more strait-laced, is illusory. A modern teacher with a large class who has eschewed formal teaching simply cannot afford anything but the most economical use of time, materials, and methods, where everything makes a contribution to the child's general education. The teaching of reading is then woven into many other classroom activities. Yet it is also taught in a systematic way with records kept of the children's progress.

Although the general arrangements may be flexible, allowing children to follow their interests, reading must be organized into a programme, although this programme will have many informal elements. A programme designed for a large class must obviously make reading as much as possible a communal activity. Reading will emerge from and be linked to, other classroom activities, for example great use can be made of attractive captioned pictures on the walls. These should be professional pictures of a high standard. Such material is unfortunately rather rare and may have to be supplemented by the teacher's own efforts. Young children's drawings are not useful for this purpose, because they are often difficult to recognize, they have limited themes, and not least, they are of little interest to the other children.

At the start the captions should be short, in letters easily visible all over the room. Interest can be sustained in a picture by the teacher discussing it or telling a story about it. The children can be asked to read the caption together and from time to time a child may be asked to pick out a word. The initial purpose is simply to get the children to understand the nature of a word as a sign, (the equivalent for adults of say, making sense of Chinese characters).

Picture captions can be supplemented by labelling of objects in the room, but when this is done indiscriminately it becomes pointless. Notices about activities and labels for display fit naturally into the classroom but the notion of labelling the door, the walls, the cupboard, the window etc. is weak and unreal. Children display little interest in these commonplace objects and there is no point in regularly drawing their attention to them. On the other hand an instructive message such as 'Please shut the door' is continuously useful. In any case all labels and captions should be frequently drawn to the children's attention or they will become part of the scenery.

Children's acquaintance with reading as a continuous activity is of course gained through listening to the teacher read. It is a good idea to use simple and colourful books from the class library, which the children can afterwards handle and 'read' themselves. This makes reading seem more attainable and at the same time if the teacher puts plenty of zest and acting into the reading, reading is a source of great fun. A further advantage is gained in reading to a small group of children, as this allows more emphasis in recognizing words and discussion of the material. Unfortunately most teachers do not have the necessary auxiliary help to get such valuable intimacy into the reading lesson. The teacher must stress the care she expects the children to take of the books, in the way she does. Some children have never been taught at home the slightest respect for books and may be tempted to tear, scribble, and snatch.

A class library for beginners needs careful organization. The emphasis should be on quality not quantity, and on attractive appearance as much as on attractive contents. Young children are lost with closely packed shelves. They dislike old and dirty books. They respond best to a few well-displayed, attractive-looking, and, above all, familiar books. It is probably a mistake to curtain off the book corner. Reading at this stage is a fairly noisy communal activity. Also a curtained-off book corner encourages other sorts of play, such as 'house-play' making supervision difficult. The visual impact of attractively displayed books is lost. Finally, the children reading the books should be in the visual range of the busy teacher.

We have seen earlier that the youngest group of children take most readily to the known and the familiar. They get pleasure from recognition rather than revelation. There is a strong argument for including in the book corner, books made by the teacher and the class. There has been a vogue for such material, to the extent that home-made books have been turned into show items which may never get read. However, when they are well made and interesting, and part of the library stock, they are highly successful. A badly-made and boring home-made book is an expensive waste of time. The ingredients of failure are unrecognizable pictures, which many children produce in their first years at school, the poor drawing of most teachers, and the difficulty of obtaining specific illustrations for particular themes.

The successful effort will come from a selective policy, where an exciting event such as a Christmas party, or a visit to the zoo, or a collection of well-loved rhymes, possibly a simplified version of a fairy story can inspire books with the appeal of successful printed ones plus the extra value of the children's proud recognition of their own work. However the cost in time and materials is very great and should be weighed against less highly organized but more profitable activity.

One of the main classroom activities is drawing pictures, then talking and writing about them. The main purpose of this is teaching writing. However, it also assists children in their reading. It does this less from the reading of their own writing than by making children aware of the shapes and structure of words and phrases. The general procedure is for the teacher to caption the child's drawing with large, clear, well-spaced words. The child can eventually come to trace over the teacher's writing and later to copy it. There may have to be some negotiation with the child to agree on a concise caption. Some children's drawings yield an endlessly detailed narrative, others only a single word. Some teachers hold to the maxim that a child's writing book should become his first reading book. This idea needs examining. The child soon forgets or loses interest in what he has drawn and written, making it difficult to sustain the use of a writing book as a reading primer. There is also a danger that the over-use of writing books for this purpose will dampen the child's enthusiasm for writing and drawing.

Children are usually interested in their own names. Advantage can be taken of this as a start to word recognition. For example, the child can be provided with a piece of thick card on which his name is printed. The children enjoy tracing their name or playing the game of finding their name amongst a pile of name cards. This can be made easier by using different colours of card.

The relentless captioning of children's paintings can do little good, even when they are used selectively for wall display. Their main drawback is that a child's painting is of little interest to the rest of the class, especially as the majority of pictures are non-representational, where the subject emerges as an after-thought. Too much attention drawn to certain subjects can result in an overwhelming vogue for the successful formula. From the teacher's point of view, choosing pictures, deciding and writing captions, and arranging displays are deceptively time-consuming activities. As a result displays of children's paintings tend to remain longer than their limited usefulness requires. In learning terms the caption format (Jane painted a . . . or a . . . by Jane) is extremely limited and is difficult to form into a developing sequence of vocabulary and ideas. Rather than using time to caption displays of children's paintings, it suits class morale and children's time sense to aim for frequent changes of displayed handiwork.

The need for good pictures

Display material to help reading clearly demands exciting, relevant, and unambiguous pictures, preferably printed in colour. The amount of material that is officially available is totally inadequate. The fallacious assumption is made that because the reading vocabulary is simple and narrow the pictures must be simple and trite. This ignores the fact that children's vision is a million times more efficient than their reading perception. In other words they are not learning to see. They have done this already. They are relating verbal symbols to the vast, complex activities that they can perceive in the world. Therefore the need is less for illustrations of the text than for stimulating and realistic material. The case for textual illustrations is weakened by the extraordinary amount of ambiguity and irrelevance in even the simplest illustration. For example, it is only by a train of association that a picture showing Jane patting the dog, the dog licking Peter's ear, and Peter pouring the dog's drink refers to 'The dog likes Jane and the dog likes Peter'. The remaining relationships are left unexplored. You are invited to 'like Peter' when he is kneeling on the grass, by the water, close to another boy, making ready his yacht, and wearing his usual immaculate clothes, including his red jersey etc. etc. Obviously a great many statements can be made about such a picture. For example, an intelligent five-year-old insisted that Peter was playing with his boat. I replied 'Yes he is, but it doesn't say that'. This is not to decry the pleasant nature of illustrations in reading books and the difficulties of illustrating a small vocabulary. However, the direct use of visual material to teach reading will demand a very flexible and definable flow of material. We may also have to accept a certain hit-or-miss quality in such pictures. What is needed is a copious supply of high-quality material, preferably including topical material, i.e. that makes sense in a child's immediate environment. There is an astonishing discrepancy between the parts of our society where there is no such supply viz: education, and the parts where there is, where the mass media of magazines and posters have accustomed us to the cheap supply of pictures. They are pictures of news, entertainment, and advertising. Some of them reach tremendously high standards of reproduction. Very often the advertising pictures are the best of all because advertisers are most meticulous about the kind of picture they want to associate with their product. It would be fallacious to imagine that advertisers can 'afford' such high quality and the educational system cannot. It is a matter of economy of means and of taking advantage of technical developments in printing and the assurance of large 'runs'. There seems every argument for taking a leaf out of the advertisers' book.

It is interesting to calculate what the market for a picture service might be and the sort of costs involved in running it at the highest standard. There are at least five million children in primary schools, and if one assumed that there were forty per class, this means that there are 125,000 classes which could make use of all or part of a regularly produced portfolio of pictures. With this length of run and a guaranteed market, the cost of full colour printing could be brought down considerably. The cost might be measurable in terms of a few pounds a week per school or picture costs measured in shillings or even pence. Related to the total costs of running a school these are very minor costs indeed. Admittedly it would take a certain amount of courage for teachers to think of an abundance of 'throw away' material, because pictures tend to be thought of in the same way as text books which are treated with parsimony. On the other hand drawing and handicraft material is disposed of as rubbish after use. What an explosion of colour and interest there could be in our classrooms with a liberal supply of good pictures, sufficiently varied in subject matter, size, and appeal to make them an important and changing part of the school environment.

With the present lack of pictures the onus is on the teacher to provide her own material or to direct the children in making pictures for reading purposes. The aim must be to produce recognizable and attractive pictures relating to subjects of interest to the whole class such as a favourite fairy story, a seasonal event, and so on.

It is a valuable exercise to incorporate the vocabulary of the early reading books into classroom illustrations. For example, notices and captions to wall pictures and models can be arranged to include words and phrases which are being studied. Children can be asked to match flash cards to these words. Children like to play 'teacher' with a pack of flash cards and will start this activity spontaneously and carry on happily for quite long periods. This gives them extra practice in word recognition even if occasionally this develops an ability to recognize words upside down!

When a reading series has central characters, as is usually the case, they may be introduced to the class by means of wall pictures. This can be done well in advance of starting reading. The teacher can make up her own stories around the characters so that they become popular with the class.

Although flash cards are very useful apparatus for teaching reading, the straightforward showing of them can become quickly boring. This can be remedied to a certain extent by devising games to be played with small groups of children, e.g. where the child wins a card if he gets the word right. Games like this can be easily rigged so that everyone gets a chance of winning and nobody is discouraged.

Thorough preparation will give the child a good start with his first reading book but it is by no means necessary to learn every word beforehand. The planned repetition of words within the book will take care of unfamiliar words. For the beginning reader, success breeds success. The achievement of being 'on' a reading book and then of finishing it, is seen as a tremendous personal triumph. The child will boast to his admiring friends and his parents. In the first flush of enthusiasm he will probably reread the book several times.

There have been enormous improvements in the volume and layout of the all-important first reading books. The number of words used in a first book has been cut down from anything above fifty, to twenty or less. Accepting for the moment the desirability of having the minimum vocabulary of basic words, it is a difficult task, as I have shown, to create meaningful test with words which can be used in later readers. The Ladybird Key Word Reading Scheme approached the problem methodically and statistically. The sixteen word vocabulary with which the scheme opens claims to include the twelve most commonly used words in the language and manages to make a fair amount of sense with them.

For infants, pictures are essential for creating and maintaining interest. In the earliest stages the pictures will completely dominate the text. Therefore the danger must be avoided of having pictures which interfere with the text. This happens when the main action of the picture and an accompanying statement are at variance. The pictures are important as they will determine the appeal and interest of the book. They should be large and colourful with a clear message.

The length of the book is also very important. A book must be capable of being read quickly, allowing the child to pass on to the next. Achievement will be judged by the excitement of finishing one book and starting another which is always a fresh incentive. It is of course the repetition of words in a book or series which is most responsible for thorough learning; but if repetition is achieved at the cost of boredom the child's learning will be hampered. A further incentive to maintain the child's interest in reading is to make sure that each time he gets a new book it really looks new. Dirty, dog-eared books are most depressing objects and put children off reading. Crisp new books with vivid and interesting covers are exciting objects that spur the class on.

Long before they can recognize words children 'read' picture books with great pleasure. They go on finding exactly the same pleasure in pictures when they can read. No child should have to face a book where the text overwhelms the illustrations or where the illustrations are small and insipid. Pictures should remain as props long after the children are fluent readers. For children, reading never becomes completely functional. Right up to teen-age children prefer books with pictures. Most reading-book publishers behave as if pictures were still very expensive in comparison with words. We live in an age where visual images are cheap. Colourful magazines are the picture books of adults. The pictures get changed every week which is more than happens with reading books, where pictures may remain for decades, becoming more and more ludicrous. In the Janet and John series Mother wearing a 1930s dress is observing the timeless progress of a biplane. Her dress length has become fashionable again but the style of the air transport is unlikely to be revived. Even if one were able to find it charming one would have to protest against images which are so dated as to be meaningless to contemporary children. Such things as these are bound to reinforce the difference for most children between the world of learning and the world of experience, in spite of recent efforts to disguise the former as the latter.

There is an astonishing contrast between the almost wilful insipidity of commercial reading text-books and the wealth of appealing illustration in children's picture books in libraries and book shops. There is no reason why artists, such as Tomi Ungerer, Maurice Sendak, John Burningham, Richard Scarry, Dick Bruna, should not be commissioned to produce material for reading textbooks. They might also stand the test of time a little better, if economy is such an overriding consideration. Perhaps even notable children's writers, including some of those mentioned above, could be persuaded to work within a 'scientifically graded vocabulary' to produce some sparkling reading books. There is a grey anonymity about even the best of the reading schemes and it is clear that too much science and too little art goes into the production of 'learning-to-read books'.

The influence of classroom organization on reading

If their content was more pleasurable and stimulating reading books might be expected to be more successful. Under no circumstances is there any necessity for books to be devoid of verbal or visual sparkle. On the other hand the teacher's classroom experience throws up some severe constraints governing the format of reading books and the make-up of reading schemes. The elements of the situation are the size of the class, the time available for reading supervision, the average mental capacity of the children, and above all the competitive spirit that acts as an incentive and provides momentum for the reading achievements of the class.

For the forseeable future it is likely that most infant classes will have thirty-five or more children 'on roll'. Allowing only two minutes per child per day for individual reading attention, this would take over an hour, which is a large slice of an infant day. It is clearly impossible to test each child adequately each day, nor is it desirable. Many teachers, conscious of the shortage of time, and trying to operate an equitable system, listen only to short fragments of reading, a page or two at a session. Such a fragment of reading will diminish the value of repetition which is the main purpose of these reading schemes, and will lack the sense which comes from context. It is far more valuable for the teacher to arrange for children to read a large amount less frequently, for example once a week. The ground covered might be a dozen pages of an average text book. A longer reading session has the advantage of allowing the teacher to judge the child's development in spite of errors. The bit-by-bit approach tends to dwell too much on individual errors.

It is inescapable that children get tremendous pleasure from passing from one reading book to the next. The more this can be encouraged, the better readers they will become. It follows from this that each reading book should be as short as is compatible with a working vocabulary. If we take into account a young child's lack of patience, the absolute limit of time spent on a reading book will be four weeks, suggesting a book of no more than twenty to thirty pages. In the end it is up to the teacher to decide exactly when the child should move on to a new book. If the child is not ready to progress it is better to move sideways or even backwards into a different series of books. These observations may seem obvious, but they are by no means universally acceptable in the teaching profession. There are still schools which concentrate on a single reading scheme unsullied by contact with rival literature. The larger issue is the uncertainty that exists about the practical application of the various reading schemes. A typical reading scheme indicates reading ages which if approximated to actual reading ages would allow six months per book! or something like three school days per page! Some schemes do provide supplementary material but the need remains for a wide choice of exciting reading material and the avoidance of a parade ground approach to reading.

Faced with the shortage of time for reading supervision, most teachers organize group reading. This saves time and may encourage some types of children but it does have drawbacks. The method depends on the group following the text with their eyes, while each child in turn reads a page aloud. The chief disadvantage is the boredom of children having to hear their colleagues read in a halting, expressionless voice. Their attention soon wanders. Assuming their turn comes round every one in five or six times they are effectively exposed to a fraction of the material. A second problem is variable ability. However well balanced the group is, the teacher cannot take into account the uneven progress of children's reading ability. A child may well wish to go on and read a whole book alone. Then he should be allowed to leave the group and progress alone. It is essential that children who are just beginning to read must read their first and second books at least individually to the teacher. Young children are essentially selfish and the whole purpose of reading for them at this stage is that the teacher should hear them and them alone.

The need for supplementary reading material

What the teacher knows least about is how learning to read takes place. This is not surprising as little enough is known in general about learning and memory. (What is surprising in primary education is the way partial theories are promoted as complete teaching methods.) What the teacher does have is continuous observation of the sudden blossoming of readers. No teacher worth his salt will take credit for this achievement any more than the gardener will take credit for the flowers, except in respect of careful preparation and careful nourishment.

To adopt a natural approach to this kind of learning must lead one to think of reading as a continuous process. In other words it follows a curve and not a series of steps. But most reading series assume a stepwise development of reading and only a few concede a grudging amount of supplementary material. It is not surprising, therefore, that if there is a measurably steep gradient between each stage some children will come to a halt. What is needed to maintain the momentum is a copious amount of supplementary material that is flexible enough to adjust to the child's progress, including backsliding. As with any other skill, practice makes perfect, but the best accomplishment comes from varied practice, and children learn to read best from continually reading varied material that presents familiar words and introduces new words. When this process is properly controlled these new words will be grasped from the context and will pass effortlessly into the child's reading vocabulary. This of course is a never-ending process that continues into adult life. In short, the more books a child is encouraged to read the more rapid and enjoyable will be his progress. The teacher's rôle is to select and control the supply of books. If the books are sufficiently interesting and exciting the child will willingly carry on alone and will graduate to a free choice of reading. If we define the teacher's rôle thus she is at present somewhat lacking in opportunities to exercise it except by ad hoc mixing of different reading schemes, and school and public library books. It is a matter of chance whether these choices are present.

The problem of finding suitable supplementary material becomes easier as the child's reading vocabulary expands. After a certain point he may be able to choose suitable material from the class or local library. At this point the transition is made from reading aloud to the teacher to reading aloud to himself which will eventually develop into silent reading. This is not to be seen as practising in advance but as self-teaching. However, the teacher must still carry on hearing the child read regularly. This is the extremely important phase where reading passes from being a purely physical skill to an intellectual activity. Providing there is enough good supplementary material, new words do not present a problem. Recognition of the word follows from the context in which it is met. The child may ask the teacher, parent, or even another child, the new word. He may work it out phonetically. The disadvantage to reading alone is the temptation to skip in order to give the impression one is getting on. This can come from boredom with the book as well as from a desire to keep up with classmates. The teacher's responsibility is to see that a child gets maximum value from a book without necessarily learning every single word.

The task is easier and pleasanter when there are interesting books. Only fanatical children will read uninspired material comfortably. Some children are extremely fastidious. Fortunately a certain amount of tasteful and interesting material appears on the market. The names that spring to mind, are the World's Work Press, Collins and Harvill's Beginner Books, and Dick Bruna's books. The point is, such books are not merely more imaginative and pleasant but they can produce electrifying results. A previously inattentive child can become unable to put down one of these books and will joyfully read it over and over again. Children can become so engrossed in a good book that they will feel annoyed at such distractions as playtime and having to go home. It is a delightful sight for the teacher when the idlest and toughest boy in the class wanders out to play while still reading his book. His subsequent rapid progress in reading is owed not to method, not to skill, but to the sheer quality of the material, the factor most often ignored by theorists.

Special Books as a reward

At present even a combination of reading schemes is too narrow to provide material that can hold a child's interest whether he is making progress or marking time. At first sight the class library ought to fill the gap. It does not for two reasons. Firstly children cannot be relied on to choose a book exactly suited to their current reading level, and secondly like any other library, not everybody uses it. Most children need the discipline of being given a book by the teacher which they can clearly see represents degrees of advance.

A successful method I have developed is to select about fifty books notable for their appeal and entertainment value as well as their vocabulary, to rank them alongside formal schemes and to issue them as appropriate under the emphatic title of *Special Books*. The books are kept in a set and are visible on a shelf and each child has a record of his reading of these books which is not necessarily in a fixed order. As the list on the child's record lengthens the child's pride increases. Partly because time is short and partly because special books are a pleasurable reward I do not listen to the children read these books but I carry out spot checks on each child.

Further uses of a flexible library of special books under the teacher's charge are firstly, the opportunity to set up ad hoc reading partnerships where a slower child can read to a more advanced child and vice-versa. This works particularly well if the children are good friends. Secondly a teacher can actually enhance the value of the books by reading selected ones aloud. Of course ordinary 'readers' should be capable of being used like this but they stand up to neither test. Children do not get excited or involved to anything like the same extent. The books that I have found successful in this rôle are once again the Collins and Harvill's Beginner Books and the 'I can read books' published by the World's Work Press, and Dick Bruna's books. The test of the suitability of such books is the unvarying eagerness with which children read them. Humour is always attractive to a child and it is the high quality of the humour of these books which makes them winners. In spite of the fact that humour is extremely rare in education or perhaps because of it, humorous books tend to be frowned on by the establishment. Learning is much too earnest a matter to be fun!

The hidden virtues of comics

In the last few years there has been a great interest in ephemeral art, namely 'pop-art'. In certain circles comics have become culturally respectable even to the extent of admiration of their visual and literary styles. Needless to say this thinking has not reached educational circles where the children's own private choice of reading material is still treated with disdain. Rather than frown on comics the teacher should assess how they may help the child's reading. Comics are variable in quality but even the worst of them use an economical vocabulary where the meanings are heavily reinforced by the illustrations. In this sense, though they may be rubbish they are better designed than the genteel rubbish of some reading schemes. The best comics on the other hand, show a lightness of touch and a verbal and visual wit which is rarely encountered in 'proper' narratives. An excellent example is the comic strip 'The Adventures of Tintin' by M. Hergé which has been collected in the form of several books. Tintin is perhaps in a class of his own since he has so many virtues, but he illustrates the advantage of the genre. This is the ability to carry a child through a complex adventure story, with a high degree of characterization, and shifts of scenery, at a pace which would be utterly outside the child's range in a written book. In this way the Tintin books can provide a massive vocabulary of people and places (including a nice line in nautical curses). Notwithstanding their undeniable quality they appear to be considered unsuitable for public libraries and schools as they have not shaken off their humble origin as comics.

To summarize the advantages of the comic form, it is the most economical way of telling a story, it uses all kinds of visual devices to retain attention, it uses conversational vocabulary. Above all it belongs to the child's world and children find comics irresistible.

Making use of the competitive spirit

Perhaps to the dismay of theorists and many fair-minded teachers one of the most striking aspects of a school class, particularly in respect of learning to read, is the strong competitive spirit that exists. Of course this is a bad thing only if there is a single race which has a few 'winners' and some very bad 'losers'. It is up to the teacher to arrange a lot of races where everybody at some time comes out a winner. Children are acutely aware of how far they have progressed in their series even when the publishers have commendably removed numbers or other signs of grading from the book.

The competitive spirit can be put to excellent use. What actually happens is that the quickest learners blaze a certain trail, which the rest of the class eagerly follows. They hope to catch up but they are not discouraged if they do not because they are able to note their own progress. Even the slowest reader who can only race against himself, i.e. noting his own progress, is happy about this, providing that the teacher shows that she is delighted at his achievements. The key factor is the enthusiasm of the teacher. Each new accomplishment must be greeted with unrestrained joy. Exceptional efforts can be rewarded with the headmistress's accolade. (One of the strains of modern teaching is the amount of joyful swooning the teacher must continually do to keep up the incentives.) However slow a child is, he must get a share of these honours.

One might ask, why waste all this time and effort on slow

readers who could perhaps be drilled to a rudimentary standard of reading? The answer must be that although they may still achieve only a rudimentary standard by the time they leave infant school, they will associate reading with pleasure and want to carry on. The alternative might be complete loss of communication and educational failure.

5 How parents can help

Why teachers find fault with parents' efforts

The question of whether parents should help their children learn to read is an emotional one. A lot of the emotion is on the teachers' side. Some teachers resent parents' efforts as interference, some are indifferent to it, but other teachers welcome it and encourage it. Thus the extent to which parents help the children in learning to read is a reflection of the teacher's attitude. It is hard to see how any interest taken by parents in their children's education can be construed as harmful or interfering. It is usually quite simple to pick out those children soon after they have entered school, whose parents are concerned with their education. These children usually know how to handle pencil and paper. They are often able to draw, a few can read or write. However, it is above all their general knowledge and vocabulary which marks them out. They have been read to, talked to, taken on holidays and visits. The whole width of their horizon is greater and they would appear to have an advantage over their classmates.

One of the signs that the parents are interested, and also one of the indications of the teacher's attitude, concerns the accomplishment some children have, when they come to school, of writing their name and perhaps the alphabet, in capital letters. This often seems to annoy teachers, who feel for some reason, that this will upset the child and interfere with his normal progress and hinder his respectable progression in lower case letters. There is not the slightest evidence that this is so. If a child can write his name in capitals it is as well to allow him to do that for the time being, for it gives him a sense of personal achievement. He will later adjust quite simply to lower case letters and will probably use both quite happily for a while.

Once a child has begun to read he will probably be pleased to take his book home and read it to his parents. This can only do good. The more a child reads, the better. The more reading aloud to parents he does, the better. Younger readers love an audience, and this gives extra practice and leads to progress. As a child gets more advanced and he can read the whole of a book to his parents, there should be no need to read that book again to the teacher. The child should be given another book. Once enthused, children can reach the stage of reading a book in an evening at home, either alone or to their parents. This practice helps the child considerably and the teacher's only difficulty is providing enough suitable books for the child to carry on taking home. Teachers have so little time in the classroom to hear children read, and there are so many activities they have to fit into the curriculum, they should be more than pleased when parents are helping, whether actively or merely passively. There are advantages to reading at home. It is likely to be much quieter and freer from distraction than the classroom, and there may be more leisurely time to talk about the book, and the subject matter.

Why then do teachers find fault with parents' efforts and refuse to allow reading books out of the school? There are indeed possible disadvantages to parents helping. These are usually due to over-anxiety on the part of the parents, a wish to see the child 'getting on'. The child may be nagged and forced to read. Reading may be generally surrounded by a dutiful atmosphere, which can put the child off to the point of hating reading. This is one of the much pleaded reasons for not letting children take books home. It is not a very sound reason. The majority must not be allowed to suffer for the unfortunate few. The children of over-anxious parents quickly become reluctant to take books home at all. If the parent becomes so insistent on forcing a child, a teacher's ban on taking books home will hardly help. Anxious parents can easily obtain reading primers from the shops, where nowadays they are encouraged to buy them. It would be far better if the teacher gained the opportunity of discussing with the parents, the reading problem of their child, especially if he comes to dislike reading.

The Ladybird Reading Scheme has been heavily merchandised and made available in many bookshops and newsagents. Parents are encouraged to buy these books in numerical order and presumably to put children through a sort of do-it-yourself reading course. This is extremely unwise, because parents will have no knowledge of the varying rate at which children learn, and will expect too rapid progress. They will not be aware of the six-monthly stages in which the scheme is drawn up, and in general will have no guidance as to how to use it. Furthermore they will have no notion of how close to the average their child is, and hence at what intervals a fresh book should be obtained. Parents who are intent upon using such schemes should do it only with the advice of the child's teacher. They should also reflect that there is a good deal more entertaining material available to read *with* the child.

Teachers as a whole are very conscious of injustice. There may be some thought that the child whose parents help him has an unfair advantage. He has an advantage, but it can hardly be called unfair, more a matter of luck. This should surely point to the wisdom of encouraging all parents to help, however difficult this task may appear. Most parents are concerned for their children's education. It would be a good idea formally to get rid of the non-interference notion once and for all. There is no suggestion here that parents should try to teach the child to read alone, or even force it to read before it is ready. This would be disastrous, but once a child is in school the best results will come from the parent working alongside the teacher. At the other extreme there is the child whose parents seem to have no time to help. This does not always mean that the child is completely without help, for sometimes an older brother or sister will help. This is not at all dangerous, because the brother or sister cannot force the child against his will. Mostly both parties enjoy the exercise. An interesting illustration of this is where in successive years I taught two brothers with twelve months in age between them. The first brother found it hard to learn to read and appeared uninterested and achieved only a mediocre standard. However he must have carefully imparted his knowledge of reading, and for that matter other subjects to his younger brother, and enjoyed doing so, for the second brother came along with a knowledge of phonics and a basic reading ability. He quickly became a keen and fluent reader. He was proud of the fact that his elder brother had taught him, and apparently the elder brother was just as proud of the teaching he had been able to do.

If a number of children take a book home this becomes a fashionable thing to do. Even children whose parents give them no encouragement whatsoever, like to take books home. If they read at home it does not matter if no one there is interested. They will get extra reading practice and a parent who does not take a great deal of interest will often supply an unknown word. Furthermore and most important, as we have stressed before, children learn to read better when they read more.

The fallacy of poor home background

Perhaps there is also something about teachers that encourages them to put people into pigeon holes. One of the most popular pigeon holes is the one labelled 'poor home background'. There is a general belief that children from such poor home backgrounds are worse readers than children from good home backgrounds. The evidence for this is rather scanty and when it exists often seems self-confirming. From the teacher's own standpoint in the classroom it is difficult to define exactly what is a poor home background and what is a good one, for the abstract definition must give way to particular cases. It is evident that a home where books are not held in respect or which lacks books altogether will be a cultural drawback to the children from that home. There again, however, we are simply providing a circular definition. The children from such a home will lack general knowledge, which assists reading. They could be slower to start reading. This is not a reason why they should not eventually make progress. It is of course the place of school to supply the books and the general knowledge and to stimulate an interest in books and the use of libraries. Perhaps those children are worse off who do get some books, which come as gifts from parents or relatives, chosen from among the synthetic rubbish that some publishers and some adults think of as children's books. These may bore the child and put him off books. If this happens, at least the child is showing some rudimentary taste. If the child can tell his parents what sort of book he enjoys, it may make the parent more aware of what constitutes suitable literature. Here the teacher must provide the stimulus.

Homes which are emotionally unstable do not necessarily impair reading progress. Without extensive data on such homes one can only generalize about them. Children from broken or apparently unhappy homes may turn out to be good readers. It is altogether possible that children are more resilient than we think. The child who grows up in an unstable home may be badly affected. He may on the other hand be less shattered emotionally than a child who has always had a stable home which suddenly and unexpectedly breaks up. Sometimes mothers who have been deserted work very hard to help their children; perhaps they are trying to compensate for their loss. No hard and fast rules can be made about broken homes, breaking homes, or unstable homes, or their effect on reading performance. Only individual behaviour emerges. Families of low intelligence may produce badly organized homes. The children's poor performance may be attributed only to physical home conditions. It may be equally true that the children have low intelligence and that this, rather than lack of a stable and happy home, will be the major factor in hindering reading and other learning. The apparently well-brought-up and cared-for child may be stifled by over-anxious parents who are too eager for their offspring to get on and do the right thing. An extreme case of this over-concern, in my experience, was that of a nervous and badly-behaved girl, who could in no way be said to be deprived, and was having difficulty in reading and writing. I found out that when the little girl left school she had tea and was sent straight to bed without being allowed to play or watch television. This was in order to be fresh for school next morning. The little girl was eventually moved to a private school in the hope that she would make better progress. The question as to how far her behaviour was inherited and how far it was the result of her environment is unanswerable, but it points up the danger of over-simple generalizations about home background.

In fact there is something to be said for more rugged living conditions. Quite often parents living in poor conditions are not houseproud and this may mean that their children have better and less inhibited play facilities. Even if they are cramped this can hardly compare with the classroom where often forty children are packed into a small room. Parents in poor housing, slums if you like, may cheerfully put a child's picture on the wall or display a junk model. Parents in smart new flats or houses are usually more concerned with appearances than their children's happiness. Children are prevented from making a mess and a picture on the wall is unthinkable.

Without idealising the street urchin he is as likely to be as well off, if not better off, than an over-protected child in a genteel home. The world after all, is a rough place and a gutter culture may turn out to be more helpful and richer than a good but sterile home environment. Again this is a matter of questioning our priorities, of *not* trying to solve educational problems with bricks and mortar. A teacher must learn to weigh up each home on its own merits, not in terms of the rather superficial judgements about home background that are currently fashionable.

Educating parents

Many parents do want to help in the education of their

children. The best way they can do this is in co-operation with the teacher, but this presupposes that they are aware of how infant education works. This is usually by no means the case. So the first problem is one of the education of the parents. They must first of all be shown how education is changing. Even for middle-class parents the changes are often presented in a gimmicky fashion. But for most parents it is a problem of allaying their anxieties. The majority of parents still worry because their children are not launched into a programme of reading, writing, and arithmetic at five years old. They see their five-year-olds going into school to play. If they are not around to see this they will be told by their offspring that he has played all day. Sometimes exasperated parents will choose a school where formal teaching still takes place so that good teaching is being 'seen to be done'. It may even be a school where a uniform proves that it is indeed an educational establishment. What is most needed is a general effort by TV, magazines, and newspapers to bring home to all parents what is happening in the infant classroom so that they can apply proper criteria to the choice of school and can understand and become involved in their children's early education. Unfortunately at the moment parents are mostly unwelcome in the infant classroom. There is a reason for this. It comes about because the teacher of a large class finds it impossible to cope with parents and children at the same time. If every teacher had a good classroom auxiliary or assistant teacher, the difficulty would not arise. Either the teacher or the assistant would be free to keep the children from getting out of hand while the other spoke to the parents and explained what was going on.

There are two classes of parents who may not find their way into the classroom during the day. There are the parents who are at work and there are also the parents who are perhaps too shy to enter a classroom. For these parents open evenings, where the parents are made to feel at home and welcome, are particularly useful. If parents can come to understand how their children are being taught they will know best how to help with their children's education. The most important thing for parents to realize is the positive method of encouragement and praise now used in the classroom. For parental criticism can be extremely damaging to the child's confidence. Those parents who are not willing to come along to open evenings will probably not want to help their children anyway. There can be no ideal solution and some children must always be the neglected ones.

The best way to help

Recently there has been a fashion for teaching babies to read by showing them 'flash' cards, i.e. a large card with a word printed on it. This is a great pity. It will probably appeal to anxious parents. For the child, at best it can be only useless, at worst it may be harmful. A toddler may very well learn to recognize a word after seeing a flash card a number of times. He may recognize a number of words but where does he go from there? There are no books written on the intellectual wavelength of toddlers or small babies. If there were could they handle such books? They would be more likely to screw them up, listen to them crackle and crinkle, tear them, chew them, and rightly so, for this would be their emotional attitude to books. Perhaps they could be trained to respect books but this must be a great strain on the patience of both parent and child. Neither nagging nor fear should be associated with reading. If the child is not at all ready to recognize words on flash cards, these will have to be continually re-presented and they will then be easily forgotten. The poor child could be bored to tears with the words. The mother could better use her time talking to him, showing him pictures, singing, or reading to him.

There is no reason at all why a parent should not teach a child to read before he starts school, providing the child is ready and able to learn and it involves no hard grind. If the child is ready he will be keen to learn and it should be a pleasure. I personally feel that very few children, particularly boys, are ready before the age of five. It would be unwise of a parent to make reading into a chore. Unless parents are absolutely sure the child is keen to learn, it is perhaps better to err on the side of leaving well alone, for no harm will come to a child from not learning before he goes to school. The time could be better spent doing other things with his parents.

What then can the parents do to help their children in learning to read? Before children go to school the best thing parents can do is to read or tell stories to their children. When children have started school, parents who want to help should approach the teacher. If a parent approaches me and the child is ready to read, I provide or recommend suitable books and I suggest short daily sessions of about ten minutes listening to the child read. I ask parents to supply unknown words and not to make the child build them up phonetically. I also remind the parent that reading must be a pleasurable activity. They should express delight at the smallest effort and they should never nag.

This is important advice because alongside ordinarily reasonable parents, I have to deal with some immigrant families, chiefly West Indian and Indian, who have a strong desire to see their children get on and set them a strict programme of homework, perhaps one or two hours a night. The result of this can be repressive and lead to the child letting off steam in the classroom, and certainly becoming inculcated with a dislike of school work.

Whether or not the teacher welcomes the parents' help, and whether or not the child is ready to read, parents should be prepared to take their children to the junior library and a good book shop to help them choose books. There are plenty of picture books and books for parents to read aloud. Children's librarians are usually tremendously helpful.

The onus is really on the teacher to help the parents, and some schools and libraries hold very useful and stimulating book exhibitions, sometimes with the aid of a local bookshop, so that books can also be bought at the exhibition.

6 Measuring progress

The call for a simple reading test

Learning to read is such a complex business and there are so many factors at work that it is almost impossible to measure a child's progress at any point in time with a single quantitative measurement. This has not deterred several people from trying to produce a scientific test, upon the result of which the teacher is asked to set great store. The reason is that there are many occasions when some form of measurement is needed. An experienced teacher will of course have no difficulty in evaluating each child's progress simply by observing him, and comparing his performance with that of the rest of the class, and against standards she has built up from previous classes. A new teacher however will need to satisfy herself that she is doing things right and will feel the need for some kind of guide to reading performance. Equally a head teacher will want to check on the progress of her children and the ability of her teachers. Administrative occasions also arise when a child's reading is measured, for example upon a change of school or a transfer to another class. Parents also will want to know from time to time how their children are getting on at reading. Finally, some kind of measurement is necessary to validate new methods of reading, experiments in the teaching of reading, and new reading schemes.

Unfortunately literacy does not lend itself to the sort of practical measurement that one can consider to measure

numeracy, agility, musical ability, manual dexterity etc. All the
attempts so far made have both theoretical weaknesses and
practical drawbacks. For a start, no one is quite sure what they
actually measure. The most commonly used type of test, which
has the attraction of being quick and simple to administer, is the
word-recognition test. The way a word-recognition test works is
as follows. The child is given a list of isolated words and asked to
read them to the tester in sequence. The choice of words and
sequence is based upon their statistical difficulty, in other words
the difficulty that other children of certain age groups have had
in reading them. On the face of it then, this test is a comparative
one and would appear to have objective validity. This soon turns
out not to be the case. The teacher can find that a fluent reader
gets a poor score and a hesitant reader is just as likely to get a
good score. The experienced teacher's judgement is often mocked
in this way. What is going wrong? Some children fail to
recognize words in such a test that they would normally be quite
capable of recognizing in their proper context.

The Schonell test

It would help to look closely at the best known and most
widely used test, which is that designed by Fred J. Schonell. It is
called The Graded Word Reading Test. It consists of ten sets of
ten words which get progressively more difficult. Each set of ten
words corresponds with a year of what is termed 'reading age'.
The starting point, the so-called initial reading age, is five years.
Before a child even attempts the test he is credited, by some
unexplained means, with a reading age of five. In fact the
starting score of five indicates a complete inability to read and
will apply equally to a child, a baby, or a block of wood. Once a
start has been made, the child is taken through the first ten
words and is allotted a reading age of six years if he can read
every word in that group, or for example, a reading age of 5·7
years if he is able to read seven out of ten. The test is
discontinued when a child fails with ten successive words.

The merits of this test are that it is quick and simple to

administer, even in the hands of inexperienced testers, and if it does nothing else it provides a rough guide to the reading ability of most children who are established readers. Its drawbacks are serious. It is insensitive at the lower end of the age scale, where the statistical chances of finding ten words from a child's limited reading vocabulary are small. At the higher end of the scale, which goes up to a reading age of fifteen years, the child is unlikely to have met the words unless he is actually fifteen years of age. They are rare words for the average adult. On this account it is also a test of general knowledge and experience. There is thus an arbitrary limit as to how well exceptionally good readers will score on the scale, unless they are capable of reading in a bold and analogous fashion. In this case they might strike lucky with words which they clearly did not understand but were able to read confidently. For this reason the test is to a large extent self-confirming and penalizes very bright young children as well as beginning readers.

This weakness is by no means restricted to the Schonell test. All similar tests of word recall depend upon an ingenious choice of words from the known vocabulary of statistically average children of the appropriate age groups. But there is no allowance made for the extreme variability of children's reading perform-ance by age and experience, which any teacher can vouch for. The specific and revealing criticism of Schonell's test is that the vocabulary has developed an archaic flavour. Few children taking the test read the word 'canary' correctly. They say 'cannery'. It simply reflects the social fact that while canaries were popular as pets some years ago their place has been taken by budgies. The more difficult selections include words very much in use but of a somewhat scholastic nature such as 'homonym', 'metamorphosis', 'judicature', 'procrastinate', and 'ineradicable'. There is something here of the pedantry and earnestness of a Victorian primer such as 'The Royal Road to Spelling and Reading an Illustrated Spelling Book in Which All the Peculiarities of English Spelling and Pronunciation are Explained on the Step by Step Principle', which was published by T. Nelson & Sons in 1867. Victorian children were asked to be familiar with such jaw-breakers as 'triglyphic', 'enneagon', 'pyrolatry', 'pyromancy', 'rabdomancy', 'lithomancy', 'oneiromancy', 'uranoscope', 'eupathy', 'psychomachy', 'sciomachy', 'odontalgia' and our old friend 'homonym'.

Another suspicious circumstance, if Schonell's test is intended to be objective, is that many of the words incorporated in the test occur in Schonell's own reading scheme Happy Venture Readers. If one analyses the test one can almost correlate each set of words to a reading book. This could be taken as evidence of the scientific nature of both the test and the books. Nevertheless it is a fact that children who are brought up on other reading schemes such as 'Janet and John', will not have the advantage of prior acquaintance with the test words, and children brought up on Happy Ventures will. This seriously weakens the plausibility of the test.

I had the opportunity of giving the Schonell test to the same three children over several years. This opportunity to 'follow through' does not often arise for an individual teacher. One child was an advanced reader who scored a reading age of 13·1 when he was seven years old. He progressed only to 13·9 in three years, though the progress of his reading habits and ability were maintained. Another child, who was reading Book Two of the 'Janet and John' series when he was seven, got no score on the test at that time, and therefore was presumed to have a reading age of 5·0. At the age of ten the same child scored a reading age of 12·9. The third child, still unable to read at eight, did not score any points on the Schonell test at eight or nine years. He therefore obtained a reading age of 5·0. When just eleven years old he scored a reading age of 11·2. Results such as this clearly demonstrate the insensitivity of the Schonell test at the lower end of the scale. The two boys who did badly at first were labelled as backward readers for the first years of their school life. Their later achievement on the Schonell test made them appear not backward, but either average or above. When a child is labelled as a result of a test of this kind it can be extremely damaging. A

83

test result which accompanies the child from teacher to teacher, and from infants to junior school, gives no clue as to his real ability or potential. Needless to say the information the Schonell test gives reflects entirely upon the child and not upon the quality of the teaching. In justifying the practical use of the test, Schonell claims 'teachers are able to use the results from the test for three things, as a basis upon which to divide their classes into sections and groups for reading, as a guide in the selection of reading books, and as a check upon the progress made by backward readers over a given period'. (Schonell 'Psychology and Teaching of Reading' page 136.)

It is unthinkable that the results from this abstract and limited test should replace the teacher's judgement in these matters. The suggestions made are absurd, revealing the pseudo-rationalism that too often puts educationists at odds with teachers. It would be difficult to imagine the choice of a book for a ten-year-old with a reading age of six, without taking into account his emotional age, his personality, his interests, his competitive spirit and his potential ability. Any reading test must either embrace these factors or clearly warn the teacher of its limitations.

The Holborn Reading Scale

The Holborn Reading Scale, designed by A. F. Watts, which is built around graded sentences rather than graded words, is unfortunately not a great advance. Even a sentence does not allow the child really to get going and the fact that the sentences are of necessity unconnected creates an air of confusion for the child. The general fault applies to this test, that the choice of vocabulary and subject matter, particularly as one goes up the age scale, is dependent on general knowledge rather than reading ability.

With a test of this nature it is occasionally possible for a very bright young child to work his way up the test and confidently to read sentences he does not understand. He does this by building up pronunciation by analogy with similar difficult words, for example words ending with -gue or -tion. Even without understanding, a child like this who can spot relationships and similarities, will have no trouble at all in becoming a very good reader. The designer of the test is quite aware of the difference between mechanical reading and comprehension and his test goes on to check the child's understanding of what he has read. In this way it is a thoughtful test, but it is spoiled by a dry pedantic approach. The sentences themselves are in a stilted antique style. Here is an example to give the flavour of what I mean. Sentence number 23, denoting a reading age of eleven, reads

'Christopher omitted to acknowledge the receipt of Michael's annual subscription.'

and the test of comprehension goes on to ask

Which of these things does it say happened? a) Michael paid and Christopher sent him a receipt, b) Michael paid but Christopher did not send him a receipt, c) Michael did not pay but he got a receipt all the same, or d) Michael neither paid nor got a receipt.

When the reader has limbered up on that one he might like to try number 32, for a reading age of 13, which goes

'These documents constitute an authoritative record of a unique colonial enterprise'. Now which of the following is correct? that a) You can trust the account given of an enterprise that was like many other enterprises, b) You can trust the account given of an enterprise that was quite unlike other enterprises, c) You cannot trust the account given of an enterprise that was like many other enterprises, or d) You cannot trust the account given of an enterprise that was quite unlike other enterprises.

I fear that tests of this nature belong more to the category of brain teasers than of proper and convenient tests of reading ability and understanding. The chief disadvantage of the Holborn Reading Scale in practice is the arbitrary means of scoring. The test is halted after children have made a total of four errors. Accomplished readers are quite capable of, indeed possibly more prone towards, making silly errors. Four slips might stop such readers in the earlier part of the test, when they were capable of going on to read the more difficult sentences with ease. A more useful way of scoring the test might be to close the test after a given number of consecutive errors.

Such tests must be regularly revised to delete dated material which is susceptible to perfectly understandable error. For example in the Holborn Reading test an unusually cultured child of ten was reading the sentence about one Leonard, who one learns has been 'engaged by the Irish Linen Association to act as their London Agent'. He read Le-onard, being more familiar with Leonardo da Vinci than the now unfashionable name of Leonard.

By their nature these tests must be negative and self-confirming. They test children's ignorance of words which remain outside their acquaintance at a certain age. They do not of course test children's knowledge of words and language within the awareness appropriate to their age. In effect they are setting up a series of hurdles which get higher and higher and the child is pulled up when the hurdles get too tough. If we can continue the analogy the small 'athletic' child, in other words the bright young reader, is at a disadvantage, although his 'athletic' ability is in no doubt. What the teacher cannot get from a test of this kind is anything very positive, anything which explores different facets of a child's ability, or explains what has gone wrong. Bearing in mind the administrative applications of the results of such tests, that I mentioned earlier, this can have an unfortunate effect if a child becomes 'labelled'.

These tests take little account of children's personality, which can have an important bearing on the test result. Bold children will attack words they have never seen before, with a fair chance of getting many of them right, and putting up their score. More timid but equally able readers will not attempt a new word, and will lower their possible score. Impatient personalities, especially those who are fluent readers, may rush at the test, ignoring all attempts at restraint and will make silly errors that would have been self correcting in context. On the other hand painstaking children will consider and read each word carefully. Children who have learned phonics may make a phonic attack on the test words and get many of them right. They could not be induced to stagger through a page of text in this way, building up each word letter by letter. Because of this it is necessary to time a reading test. Some tests do not have any time limit and therefore cannot reflect the child's fluency in normal reading. It is not proper for a child to be credited with a reading age in which fluency plays no part. The ostensible reason that tests are not timed is to avoid giving the child the feeling that he is under pressure. There is no need for the obtrusive use of a stop watch but the tester should use his judgement.

An attempt to provide diagnostic tests

Many people share my reservations about the use of tests based on word recall but these are still widely and influentially used. There have been various attempts to make up for the inadequacies of word recognition tests by the use of diagnostic tests. These are tests which not only assign a reading age to a child but try to find out in what way a child is falling behind the average and even to suggest a remedy. In this respect they are well meant but unfortunately do not succeed. There are still no simple answers to the problem of failure. There are still no simple methods for new and inexperienced teachers to turn to when their children fall behind in reading. Even for experienced teachers the anguish remains of the children who fail. How disappointing it is that in spite of their aspirations, the leading exponents of reading tests reach a point where they shrug off the main problem. For example in their authoritative work 'The Standard Reading Tests', J. C. Daniels and Hunter Diack who have managed during the course of the book to create the impression of actually knowing what they are talking about, then put the onus on the teacher by calling for 'a detailed qualitative diagnostic interpretation of the test responses'. Such a qualitative interpretation is described as 'an art which the teacher gains by judiciously blending teaching experience and the scientific understanding of the nature of the skills involved in fluent reading'. What does that mean?

The various tests presented by Daniels and Diack show a certain emphasis on phonics which is perhaps not surprising as the writers are the authors of the Royal Road Reading scheme, a phonic method. In general their remedies for any particular reading ill are vague and unspecified. These tests are not intended for children who are not having particular difficulties with their reading. Yet I am almost sure some good readers would fail certain of the tests. It is assumed nevertheless that children must score eighty to a hundred per cent in each of the tests before they can make normal progress in reading. Towards the end of the book the authors throw out a hint regarding the only way of helping a child 'who has mastered the skills of reading but who either does not wish or does not understand how to utilize the skills and therefore must be regarded as backward'. They say 'children need right from the start, interesting graded supplementary reading material which they are induced by various incentives to read for themselves. It is also essential to have some method of ensuring that the books are really read. It must however be a method that does not make reading a drudgery, which the child feels is to be resisted whenever possible'. This is very much the theme of my book and I am inclined to feel that if these writers had developed their suggestions further they might have become concerned as much with prevention as with cure.

The Neale Analysis of Reading Ability

By far the best test I have met is that by Marie D. Neale called 'The Neale Analysis of Reading Ability'. It lays more emphasis on context and is more realistic by virtue of providing a number of pages of prose which tell a little story, with an accompanying illustration. For the test the child is allowed to look at the picture (but the manual warns, not for too long) in order to become interested in the anecdote he is to read. The child is unlikely to give these rather limp line drawings more than a cursory glance and this is a pity for the idea is a good one, and could be improved by making the pictures better and more colourful, thus giving the child a better incentive to read the story. Because this method brings in both meaning and syntax I believe it gives a much fairer assessment than the recall of isolated words or phrases. The child is allowed a generous sixteen errors per page before the test is stopped. This is a good principle but unfortunately in this case there is insufficient explanation of how the scoring system is justified, beyond the arithmetical convenience of making the maximum points one hundred. The Neale test suffers from the usual failing that in the later stages it is measuring general knowledge and experience as much as reading ability, thus handicapping the younger reader. The author has gone to great lengths to correlate her test, not only with age, but with a range of other tests and there seems to be invariable correlation with these other tests. This presumably means that they all correlate with each other. This sort of result seems to remove the necessity for any initiative in designing a new test! It is surprising that theorists like Marie D. Neale who criticize the existing tests should be so anxious to show how well her improved test is aligned with the conventional ones. While standardization is necessary it must take into account different ages, different abilities, and the differences between boys and girls, since the results of these tests consistently show boys in a poorer light, up to the age of ten.

The Southgate Group Reading Test

Finally I should mention Vera Southgate's Group Reading Test. This is a good test of its kind but has the same drawback as all group reading tests. The children are put into an artificial test atmosphere by having to be seated with paper and pencil, at such a distance from their classmates that will prevent them from copying. Children in the modern infant classroom, with its mixed activities and movement, are disconcerted when they are suddenly put into such formal conditions as sitting still in one place, and carrying out orders. This is thoroughly alien to them. They do not understand why they cannot talk to their neighbours, because normally while they work in class they chatter a good deal and nowadays teachers encourage children to help each other. It is not considered copying but co-operation and exchange of ideas. The author claims that the unique advantage of group reading tests is the speed and ease of administration. But if it is necessary to spend time getting children used to test conditions, this is no advantage. There do not appear to be any other advantages to testing children's reading in batches.

Reading age and book numbers

When life was simpler a few years ago, reading books themselves had a built-in indication of reading standards. This was rough and ready and had arisen more by accident than by design. Book One of any reading scheme was likely to be more or less equivalent to Book One of any other scheme and so on through Book Two and Book Three. Teachers could exchange information about children's reading progress by referring simply to ability to read a certain number of books. This was true for Janet and John, Happy Ventures, Beacon Readers, and so on. Recently new schemes have entered the market which have caused the collapse of this rough but useful code, by introducing completely different gradings. The Ladybird series when it was first introduced, threw a number of teachers off guard, for Ladybird Book Three is more likely to be equivalent to Janet and John Book One than the then accepted Book Three standard. Teachers got the temporary illusion that children were making faster progress than in fact they were. Teachers have adjusted, but nothing has replaced the old rules of thumb. Ladybirds have at least made an independent attempt to give a suitable reading age to each book number and this in itself is helpful in giving the teacher some measure of the child's progress. The teacher accepts that if a child can read Ladybird Book Three fluently, he has a reading age of five and a half, since Ladybird allot six months of reading age per book number, starting at Book One with a basal reading age of four and a half. Unfortunately, they do not explain on what assumption these regular intervals are based, but it clearly does not correlate with the standard reading tests previously mentioned. In fact infants who get as far as Ladybird Book Ten or beyond – in other words who could claim a Ladybird Reading Age of nine, more usually score about seven on the Schonell test. This does not necessarily invalidate the Ladybird grading but shows once more the need for some kind of practical standardization. It would be better for this not to be carried out by the authors and publishers of a reading scheme, who would remain under suspicion of vested interest. My suggestion is for an independent body, possibly sponsored by the Ministry of Education, but made up of practising teachers, to look at the whole problem of standardization of graded readers and reading tests.

Until the inadequacies of the existing tests are overcome, I feel most strongly that if a child has to be given any formal grading or progress report, say to pass on to another teacher or school, it should be in the form of a written assessment by his own teacher, which covers his reading ability, his attitude to reading, and the level of the named reading scheme he has reached. Those teachers who do not use reading schemes in the conventional way can indicate the equivalent graded reader that the child would be capable of reading. Useful as it is to have a report from another teacher, the new teacher will want to find out for herself what the child's capabilities are. In any case, a child usually precedes his record by some time if he comes from another school, just when he is an unknown quantity. The child himself will often have a good idea of what he has been reading, but if he is not clear, the teacher can quickly find out by asking him to read extracts from one or two books of varying difficulty.

Head teachers may wish to assess a child's reading ability as a check on the teacher as well as the child. This may be done by the child paying a visit to the head teacher to read a reading book or to take a reading test. This may be inhibiting for even these days a headmistress can appear as an aloof and formidable figure. Reading to the head can be an ordeal which puts some children in a fright. A head can just as easily gauge how well her children and teachers are doing by creating an atmosphere of reward for hearing children read, or for over-hearing children read to their teacher.

Reporting to parents

Parents naturally want to know how their children are getting on at reading. The best way of letting them know is a verbal report from the teacher, for as we have seen, reading ages and test results can be misleading even for the teacher. They would be meaningless to the parents. If a child is making good or average progress, and by definition this applies to the majority of the class, the teacher has no problem in telling the parents. If the child's progress is slow, the teacher should be genuinely reassuring. She can explain how there are more late starters than failures. Boys, as we have mentioned, cause most anxiety. Parents should be warned that boys are often slow at reading in the early years, and that they should not be compared with their sisters. Infants teachers will always hesitate before classifying a child as dull or educationally subnormal, unless there is a complete lack of response across the whole range of subjects and activities. In reading as in other things there are plenty of children who confound pessimistic forecasts about them. Children who make no progress in infant school may blossom out in junior school. Where there is a risk of slowness in starting that embarrasses the child to the point of inhibition and refusal to read, the teacher will advise the parent to be as sympathetic and tactful as possible. The parent in turn has every right to expect that the teacher has tried all the tricks of the trade, and has not relied simply on the success or failure of a single method.

7 The library

Even after the much-vaunted revolution in infant education, the importance of libraries in the school and outside the school has not been sufficiently realized. Education often seems to proceed as if huge changes had not taken place in the world, as if all that is known was still within our capacity to know. The main problem is still seen as the acquisition of facts rather than learning where to find out, how to find out, and how to connect facts. For these reasons learning how to use a library should not be a side issue but one of the prime functions of early education. We no longer sit at a desk in the infant classroom in order to learn things by rote, and we no longer go on to learn by rote enough facts to equip us for a job. Most adults can now make superior comments about 'reading, writing, and arithmetic' but possibly feel uneasy about what has taken their place. Anyone who is honest with himself recognizes that what he has learned in order to pass an exam or even to pass the time at school has fallen from his mind. He has to look it up.

If we treat reading as a separate compartment we tend to allow a child to use a library or books of reference only when a certain stage of competence has been reached. Reading has been achieved and the child can pass on to amassing facts. But how much more rewarding to see the reading process from the start as a pleasurable information-gathering activity. Even before a child has begun to learn to read he should have access to a lot of books, and in the classroom there should always be a group of children working together with books, rather than for example doing some mechanical and useless exercise to keep them quiet. The way it works is as follows. The children ask the teacher a question she cannot answer (no teacher should be ashamed of admitting she does not know something). 'Let's try and find out together' she suggests, and here the quest through books can begin.

Such fact-finding activity is not restricted to those who can read. The library can be a good source of picture information for non-readers. For example a small boy wishes to paint a fish. He knows only of one kind of fish. A fish. He is excited and delighted to find a book on fish. He looks at it and goes away to paint many kinds of fish. He is not copying anyone. This is the first time that he has become aware that many kinds of fish exist.

Although there is little room in the classroom itself for a full library of reference books, there should be a selection of well chosen books, especially those with exciting and well-produced pictures. Children love to find pictures of things they have been discussing in class. For example a small group of five-year-olds who have been looking at an acorn are delighted to find a picture of one in a book about Autumn. They proudly show their teacher their find and excitedly call their friends to look. They are getting pleasure precisely out of the way information is stored, the way information can come from experience. Will this kind of pleasure endure? Unfortunately this is doubtful. There is no reason why children, when they become good readers, should not be self-teaching if they are shown how to handle suitable reference books. Any subject the class, or a group of children, choose to study can be thoroughly explored in books. The need is for clear, colourful, comprehensive literature that deals with a large range of subjects in an economical way. This sort of book is difficult, but by no means impossible, to find.

Of course the school library is to be seen, not only as a source of weighty study but also as a source of fun, of light reading as well as literature, for young readers. The school library should be used to supplement the restricted diet of a reading scheme from the earliest possible stage. If children can be transferred from a reading scheme to an equivalent series of library books, then so much the better. Children's books are getting more and more exciting; authors of stature are bringing out books which put the formulated reading scheme material and its derivatives very much in the shade. The class and school library should be stocked with the best. The taste should reflect that of the children not just that of the teacher. Even if the classroom is well-stocked with books, and the school has a library, children should be taken on class visits to the local children's library. This is especially important where only a small proportion of parents encourage their children to join the local library. Children will learn through school where the library is, how to use it and what a valuable source of entertainment it can be. Apart from books, children's libraries frequently offer extra-mural activities such as lectures, films, and competitions. They can add richly to the social life of the community. A children's library reflects the personality of the children's librarian, much as the classroom reflects the personality of the teacher. If the librarian is welcoming, helpful, cheerful, and understanding of children's needs, children will go more willingly than if she is severe and unfriendly. Many small children are too shy to ask for the librarian's help or they become stuck in their choices. A good children's librarian will come and talk to children in the library even if she has not been sought out. This is of course in contrast to the adult library where this might be thought of as needless interference. Yet such a small proportion of people use libraries and they are often such uninteresting places that perhaps the extension of some of the ideas that are now emerging in children's libraries might improve and enrich our existence.

8 Immigrant children

Many British cities now have a large immigrant population. Moreover there is a tendency for immigrant families to live in the same areas. Some schools then get a high ratio of immigrant children which can sometimes rise to a figure of seventy per cent. However, there is no single clear-cut problem associated with immigrant children. The difficulties of immigrant children vary according to their origin, race, and age. Very young immigrant children, whatever their race or colour, are cheerfully accepted by their classmates. The social problem of integration does not arise in infant school. Prejudice it seems, lies only with the parents. To describe a classmate as coloured or black is not in any way derogatory and friendships cut across all barriers. The only incident of racial friction I encountered in an infant classroom was between Turkish and Greek Cypriots. Most of the time they worked and played together happily, but occasionally when a quarrel did break out, racial insults came into it, with other children taking sides. This was obviously a reflection of the deep and bitter feelings expressed at home by the parents at the time, over the particular issue of Cyprus, as opposed for example to any background of prejudice.

West Indian children rarely present a language problem. Whether or not they have been born in this country their native language is English. If they have come directly from the West Indies they are likely to speak English with a strong dialect that is not always easy for the teacher and classmates to understand. Usually within a matter of weeks they adjust, and their speech grows more like that of the local children. In any case the West Indian dialect and intonation is no more of a barrier to learning to read than is cockney for example. Cockney children have the same kind of difficulty with phonics and will insist on writing 'a cap of tea', rather than 'a cup of tea'.

Children may well come from Asia, Africa, or the Mediterranean without a knowledge of the English language. The great majority of them learn to speak English very quickly, providing they are outnumbered in the classroom by English-speaking children.

The only serious trouble they experience is their initial distress at being thrown into a babbling mob that they cannot understand. They learn as much from other children as they do from the teacher. Teachers do not have the difficulty that might be expected with non-English speaking children. At first, gestures and facial expressions help a great deal in getting understanding, but in general children under eight years old in a normal classroom learn to understand English extremely rapidly, in my experience within three months. Within such a period most of the non-English speaking children I have come across have made a start at speaking English. I have known some who had begun to read by the end of three months. A striking observation is the fact that non-English speaking children never address me, the teacher, in their native language. There is only silence until the necessary words of English have been learned. My reaction as a teacher on hearing their first words of English is absolute delight. Sometimes it may also be a bit of a jolt, as when I overheard one Pakistani boy come out with his first English phrase 'I'll bash you up'. I do not subscribe at all to the theory that it is unwise to teach immigrant children to read until they can speak English fluently. I find that teaching such children to read helps their spoken English. It is entirely a matter of ability. For example I have had children speaking English only in the classroom, going home each day to a family where their native language is spoken exclusively and yet who learn to read faster than some of their English classmates. In such cases their reading may be better than their colloquial speech.

There is another myth to the effect that immigrant children hold back English children. This could only be true if there was an overwhelming majority in the class which was non-English-speaking, which is not generally the case. In my observation immigrant children can add a great deal to the cultural and educational standards of the class by bringing in a variety of personalities, skills, and abilities. For all these reasons it is quite wrong to isolate non English-speaking children in special, smaller classes. They may benefit in any case from more personal attention from the teacher, but what really counts is the large amount they pick up from other children. Young children may not feel compelled to listen to the teacher all the time, but they will be anxious to communicate with their classmates and will succeed, even though the English they acquire may be less than perfect.

The position changes quite a lot with children over the age of eight who enter school without spoken English. They are at a more serious disadvantage both socially and educationally. They will be more sensitive to the mockery that may greet their first attempts at the new language. The older the child the farther behind he will be in the curriculum. Most children can overcome this more serious handicap, but some are going to require special treatment, either individual teaching or group teaching, in order to catch up.

At this point my general plea for more attractive material for beginning readers becomes a technical need for suitable beginning material for children who are not only self-conscious about babyish material but who will find a great deal of the context of primers incomprehensible. The attempts I have seen to provide reading material for immigrant children have had the weakness of harping too much on racial harmony. For instance the Wheaton series 'Living Together' has a series of titles that sound like tracts. 'We are Friends', 'Friends in School', 'Fun in the Playground', 'Friends in the Country' etc. This sort of book draws attention to differences instead of treating them as merely incidental, and it is difficult to see why this is thought to be a useful theme for reading books.

9 Remedial reading

Borderline children who benefit from painstaking treatment

The fact has to be faced that certain children will never learn to read and write because they lack the mental equipment. However, there are a great many marginal cases, who can be brought to literacy by a more personal or painstaking approach. This group benefits from what is known as remedial reading. There are no special techniques for remedial teaching. There is usually a more intensive dose of what the teacher normally gives. These borderline children could not possibly learn to read in the time available in the classroom situation. Remedial groups are smaller and take the work at a slower pace. Their existence depends on the availability of staff (often part-time teachers who specialize in this work) and the necessary classroom accommodation. Thus they are often ruled out in the areas which need them most desperately. The situation is complicated by the parallel need to teach reading to non-English-speaking immigrant children. As noted, before the age of eight these children usually have no difficulty, providing there is a majority of English-speaking children in the class. Older immigrant children may have to be taught in a remedial group from time to time.

It is most important that remedial groups should be taken to a quiet place free from distractions for their reading lessons, as lack of concentration is often a factor in reading difficulties.

The need for remedial teaching has to be assessed differently with each group. There can be no set approach. For example with five-year-olds, failure to read is not serious and should be ignored, provided children are given adequate medical examination to check sight and hearing. When the children are six to seven a large proportion of the class is likely to have made a start at reading. A sizeable minority will not. Then it is time to give serious thought to helping those that cannot. Perhaps the best candidates for help at this age are those that are obviously intelligent but are ebullient and lacking in concentration. Such children will benefit from surroundings free from distraction as long as the reading material is exciting enough. Also those children who fall behind after long absences will benefit. There is no point at this stage in wasting limited resources in hammering away at those children who are not bright enough or otherwise not yet ready to read.

Children of seven to eight years on the other hand are approaching the end of their infants school career and most of them should have made a start at reading. That is the time to make a thorough and systematic attempt to help those that cannot read by special group teaching, which one might formally call remedial reading. Unfortunately because children are promoted to the junior school in annual batches, the age range of a batch will be 'just seven' to 'just eight'. Those who suffer from this rather inflexible arrangement are those who have just begun to read, which is more likely to contain an appreciable number of the younger end of the group. Continuity is frequently lost. It might be better to delay entry to the junior school till all the children are eight, or to have more flexibility and retain just those children who would definitely benefit from an extra year in the infant school. In any case there should be more continuity between the infant and junior school and more co-operation between the infant and junior staffs, which is often non-existent even when the schools are in the same building.

A really intensive effort should be made with non-readers in their earliest years in the junior school especially since they become more aware of their failure as they get older. They begin to feel frustrated and inferior. The reading material is even more inadequate than when they were small children and they feel affronted by anything which appears babyish. Some children will become apathetic and some alienated, while a few will continue the struggle.

TV reduces dependence on reading

When the printed word was the major means of communication, aside from the spoken word that is, then obviously reading skill was of crucial importance in terms of the knowledge and culture one had, as well as of one's job prospects. Audio-visual media provide ways of learning things, of acquiring skills, of understanding ideas, of appreciating things which depend very little on the printed word. A misunderstanding in education is that TV and radio must be adapted for educational purposes. We have radio for schools; we have had it for decades. We now have TV for schools and closed-circuit TV. All these activities miss the point, which is one that Marshall McLuhan makes very forcefully, that TV in itself is the educative force. It is the nature of TV that is affecting the way that people view the world. McLuhan raises controversy because he says in effect that the content of TV is much less important than its structure. (The medium is the message.)

When we consider TV content in a more conventional manner, the really striking thing is that it represents a vast amount of material that would otherwise have been totally inaccessible without reading facility. Even pictures have to be explained by captions. It must have been true that outside a folk culture where people pass on crafts and stories and knowledge, reading opens the door to life. Now a child who views TV is exposed to enormous chunks of both reality and fantasy, which quite overwhelm the modest amount of printed information that he might consume. In practical terms one is not absolutely dependent on reading. The child who makes very slow progress at reading can still be educated to an extent which was not possible a few decades ago. This means that we must bring up to date our ideas on the function and role of reading. Teachers involved in the problem of poor readers must surely find some consolation in the fact that such children are not cut off from sources of education, amusement, and enlightenment. At the lowest level TV provides a stimulus which was not there before. The poorer the home environment the greater value TV has. One remains suspicious in any case of the ease with which failure in reading or in any other field is attributed to poor home environment. The truth is that most home environments are lacking in some respects. Many children with classically poor environments have no difficulty whatsoever with their education.

The vital need for extra help

Any remedial teacher who believes in a theoretical external factor which prevents children from reading is doomed from the start. The remedial teacher has to be a complete pragmatist and must use and experiment with any device or aid she feels might help. The remedial group must be supplied with the greatest number and variety of simple books. In addition many of the aids that may have been discarded in the normal classroom as being too time-consuming, or requiring too much supervision, could be used more profitably with remedial groups. For example simple word games can be used, such as word lotto, snap, or word matching. The emphasis should be on games rather than exercises, so that the continual looking and saying of the same words can be made fun. If as we imagine, children learn to read in different ways then some children who are not succeeding with 'Look and Say' may benefit from phonic teaching in the remedial group, providing it is also made into a game. In short anything which brings success should be used.

The most important single factor is shortage of time. If every slow reader could have an extra ten minutes of personal attention each day it would produce spectacular results. In practice this is not possible for any teacher. Teachers need help. In the absence of sufficient qualified help the teacher could make great use of intelligent adults who could hear the children read.

Schools which have recruited voluntary aid for this job have had highly successful results. Unfortunately they have run into objections from the unions. Listening to children read does not need particular training and skill. It needs patience, sympathy, and understanding. It is exactly the sort of help that many parents give in any case. Regrettably such help is not usually available in the districts where it is most needed. Schools in middle-class districts could more easily recruit suitable parents for this sort of job. The success of this idea would depend on parents who were temperamentally suitable, who were willing to co-operate and take instruction from the teacher, and who were able to win the respect of the children. This combination of qualities is not all that common. One could see the danger of a well-meaning but domineering mother who might overwhelm a young teacher straight from training college. This sort of situation could be safe-guarded against by a system including a short period of training, along with reasonable payment. The unions are understandably sensitive about letting unqualified or semi-qualified staff into the classroom, who might ultimately take over from the teacher. I am in no way advocating this, but unions and authorities have to come to terms with the problem of shortage of staff. They must either press urgently for more fully trained staff or develop an auxiliary service as I have suggested.

Unquestionably the greatest single cause of failure remains the distressingly high pupil to staff ratio which means that in subjects like reading the teacher is often doing little more than managing.

I do not intend to deal with educationally subnormal children in this book. However I must emphasize that before a child is described as illiterate or subnormal he should have a thorough medical check on eyes, ears etc. and every effort should have been made to capture his attention with suitable reading material.

10 Criteria for an ideal reading scheme

The high price of standardization and economy

I now want to draw together my various criticisms and observations on typical reading schemes and methods, and my positive suggestions for new approaches to the problem. The responsibility for coming up with something new and better lies with writers and publishers. I rather think fresher and more suitable reading material will come not from any extraordinary new blueprint but from a more honest outlook all round, backed up with convincing 'consumer research'. As a user of reading schemes I feel I am in a similar position to the housewife with her domestic appliances. She is not in a position to redesign them but she can tell the makers what the really bad faults are, what improvisations she is making and what tasks she has to cope with. My next chapter after this will review the 'best buys', those books and series which have proved reliable in coping with different stages of the reading problem and, moreover, have remained popular with both children and teacher.

The development of a child in his first years at primary school involves dramatic and rapid changes. There are tremendous emotional and intellectual changes between the ages of five and seven. Being able to read is not necessarily connected with these changes and this creates a problem that the typical reading scheme does not take into account. Most reading primers, in content and style, are graded for a start at five. The younger the child the less critical he is of the material and the more simple pleasure he gets from recognizing words. The five-year-old gains physical delight in reading for its own sake. He reads his book aloud over and over again, pointing to each word with his finger.

The older child, especially of seven years or more, who has not begun to read, finds the available material much less enthralling. The intellectual content may be below him. The emotional values leave him cold. He is not thrilled at the sight of a blue aeroplane and he does not have to be reassured by the looming figure of Mummy. It is not simply on this account that the primer is babyish, it is also known to be babyish by the scornful classmates who read it long ago. This is a very high price to pay for standardization and economy in textbooks. The late readers we are discussing are not problem children. They may even be very intelligent and alert. The most probable explanation for their lateness is their impatience and lack of concentration. This would reinforce the need for really attractive and compelling reading material. If the child finds that, his reading does not make him want to read on, he is going to find more interesting things to do. A few children may persevere with their boring primers for the sake of catching up with their classmates. But the very need for perseverance underlines the inadequacy of the material.

The problem becomes even more acute towards the age of nine or ten when the disparity between the content of primers and the child's own experience and vocabulary, is glaring. The child feels self-conscious and again will probably be ragged about his 'babyish' books. Nine- and ten-year-olds are rightly insulted by pictures of small children, babies playing ball, and shopping with mother, etc.

There may be old-fashioned moralists who would argue that reading primers should encourage perseverance and that children must concentrate and exercise patience, and that their tastes and feelings should not be pandered to. But the fact that an appreciable number of children leave school illiterate, and that many others will never touch a book again, would seem to suggest that a wider reading material might bring its rewards.

Coming to terms with life as it really is

I have been discussing the flexibility that would have to be brought into a reading scheme in order to make primers appealing to the emotional and intellectual needs of different age groups. However it is clear that existing reading schemes are inadequate in many other directions. An ideal reading scheme with any pretensions to educational power and efficiency would have to come to terms with cultural, environmental, social, sexual, and – these days – racial factors. This is simply to say that it should come to terms with life as it really is and cease to reflect the wilfully prim and irrelevant world of Janet and John and Dick and Dora, who bore the children and grate on the teacher.

Certainly up to the age of seven the child's world has no clear cut line between fact and fantasy. The ingredients of his existence are fantasy (which may come from fairy tales, myths, and traditions) plus the experience of his immediate environment and his general knowledge, i.e. facts which he cannot vouchsafe but is asked to take on trust. He probably will not distinguish very well between these elements. Early reading schemes include some diluted fantasy, some social 'facts' but almost nothing that reflects the life of this child, in this school, in this place, at this time.

The importance of this is not so much a criticism of something that is not real. Children enjoy things that are not real. It is important because until he can read fluently a child cannot read about what is not familiar to him. He cannot make the double mental effort of both making sense of words and making sense of unfamiliar concepts. The fact that these unfamiliar concepts could include a steam engine, a school cap, and an ankle-length dress must have escaped the present day compilers of reading books.

Where to look for fresh source material

What may have started as a comfortable, romanticized reflection of middle class, suburban-cum-country life is now almost an alien fantasy. The normal environment of the majority of children these days is an urban one. Town infants know little about the country, yet reading books are full of farms, pigs, rabbits, and chicks etc. treated as familiar objects. There is little attempt to bring in the town landscape, town objects, and town events. Even the urban things which are brought in are terribly out-of-date. Whereas other classroom activities, particularly mathematics, are very close to real life, reading books are still cut off from it. It is not only in the classroom that children's knowledge and experience are being extended, the other main agent is television. The sheer volume and variety of TV material that children absorb far outweighs anything that they get from books at this stage. It is a powerful source of both astonishing fact and astonishing fantasy. Because TV material is both variable and changeable it is difficult to harness it for reading, although there is no reason why a super-hero like Batman or Tarzan should not replace the effete middle-class families. The arguments against TV and for books tend to be moral and aesthetic rather than technical.

The two main influences in a small child's life are his immediate environment and television. Yet neither of these is exploited for reading purposes although it is essential that the content of first reading books should be familiar. Only when the child is a confident and fluent reader can books be used for finding out about the unfamiliar.

Most early reading books in use today assume that their readers are middle-class with lives conforming to an outdated suburban pattern. Most children are not middle-class and the patterns of people's lives are changing rapidly with our increasing technology. The children who suffer most from these reading books are the poorer town children. TV is probably the most important cultural factor in their lives. Their homes are usually without books and their parents may not have much time to talk to them, especially if the mother is working. This does not mean that they are deprived children. On the contrary they are likely to be well looked after, well-loved with lives as full as those described as coming from good home backgrounds. Children from so called poor home backgrounds may grow up more resilient and better acquainted with human nature than more protected children. The notion of bad home background being a hindrance to education is a political one. Educationally it is an admission of failure, i.e. we cannot educate these children pending urgent social reform. It seems provisionally easier to take into account existing social conditions and design the material and techniques accordingly.

The completely unarguable difference between children is the difference between sexes. Boys like excitement and adventure in their reading. Girls are happier than boys when reading about domestic life. This must be a contributory factor to the earlier reading successes of girls, reinforcing their physical aptitude.

Immigrant children are a special problem. Often the only English they know is what they learn at school and they go home to speak their natural language. Even the slightest general knowledge cannot be taken for granted. Whether English-speaking or not, their customs and background vary enormously, and the homely type of early reader is most unsuitable for these children. Even home may be very unlike a typical English home. Even the Ladybird Key Word scheme which portrays domestic life in an up-to-date manner can puzzle small immigrant children. I recently found a group of five-year-olds of mixed races puzzled by 'Peter and Jane' dragging a large object called a tree around. Then Christmas came and a Christmas tree was duly put in the school hall. They came back to the part of the reader overcome with excitement at finding just such a Christmas tree in their book.

For immigrant children alone it is going to be necessary to recast basic reading material for infants and show how this material can be extended in the classroom to suit individual racial groups.

Even the most superficial observer would find the bulk of reading material grotesquely out of date but even the best has a narrowness of approach based on stereotypes of family life and a prim sense of what should or should not appear in a reading book.

Building on what children have in common

I have tried to show the need for fresh source material intended for beginning readers, to be more stimulating and relevant to the modern child. It may seem impossible to cater for all the different types of children we have discussed, although our educational system is beginning to recognize the variety of problems that have to be solved. Limited financial resources are always going to make for standardization. The best way of solving this dilemma is to look at what children have in common. The logical starting point is school itself. Young children's pleasure in recognizing themselves, which misfires in the current primers, could be captured in realistic portrayal of classroom activities, with identifiable people and scenes. The grounding and reassurance should come from this type of reading about the school community. Such reassurance need not always be about nice things. Children would enjoy reading about other children who fall in the playground and get hurt, about bullies who have to be dealt with, about things getting lost. Children especially love to feel virtuous when the naughty child gets his retribution, whether it be 'Struwelpeter', 'My Naughty Little Sister', or 'Bad Harry'.

Once the child has a working vocabulary from the 'real life' classroom reading he can extend his reading activity to fantasy. There are two approaches to enjoyable fantasy reading. The first rich source is the store of well-loved folk stories and fairy tales which lend themselves to simplification. Most of them do because their plot and characterization have stood the test of time. I am justifying them as beginner material not because they are merely simple little tales. Their usefulness is in linking their telling to their reading. The teacher tells and retells the favourite stories. The child's reading pleasure comes from reliving the telling. This means that at a very early stage the child is grasping the descriptive and dramatic power of language which more flatly realistic material would not provide. The archaic language which appears in some fairy tales is no barrier to reading progress, when it has been made familiar by telling. The advantage of traditional stories is that they are very good stories, and provide an excellent incentive for reading. The children eagerly look for their favourite stories. When I have given children Happy Venture readers they immediately search for 'The Three Little Pigs' and 'The Tar Baby', frequently attempting to skip the more ephemeral material.

There are two other important things that children have in common. One is television, the other is a sense of humour. Even the poorest homes nowadays have a television and children are, of course, keen viewers. TV heroes whether flesh and blood, puppets or cartoons, could provide an endless source of reading material, especially for boys. The difficulty is that they are not permanent. But the adventures of an archetypal super-hero could well form the basis of a reading series that would take care of the fantasy adventure needs of young children. A reading scheme such as this would be even more successful if our super-hero were brought to life on television in the school itself.

I will not enter into an argument about the cost and viewing facilities in an infant school as TV is spreading to most schools and the concept of TV education is widely accepted. The principal argument surrounds the moral and cultural aspects. Some people feel strongly that education should not acquiesce to pop culture. Here we would say along with General Booth 'Why should the devil have the best tunes?' Why should we not make use of media and methods which are part and parcel of the child's life though they were not at all of their elders, and make use of the themes that the children never stop talking, drawing, and writing about? If literacy is the prize, the price seems worth paying. The justification for making children literate as rapidly as possible is that it gives them a good foundation for all other school subjects.

To say that all children have a sense of humour is really to say that they all share an appreciation for zany fun and knockabout farce. They are not critical like many adults of whimsy and illogicalities providing the elements of a humorous situation are recognizable. In terms of reading books the highest success is reserved for those books which manage to do just this. P. D. Eastman's books in the Beginner book series are a notable example. In 'Go Dog Go' the riotous party held by dozens of dogs in a tree shows how simple ideas can be combined in an appealing way. The virtuoso performance in this field is by Dr Seuss in 'Hop on pop' who has shown that even the sedate 'cat on the mat', long ago dismissed by reading teachers could turn up fantastically comic possibilities and become a powerful educational force again.

It is clear from this discussion that there is no fixed time at which a child is ready to read. Each child will differ for reason of temperament, culture, and home background. In some areas the majority of children will be familiar with books and treat them respectfully. A few may already have been taught to read. In others most children in a beginning class may never have handled a book, had a story read to them, or even have used pencil and paper. In the latter case it is the teacher's responsibility to create an environment in which reading can become a desirable accomplishment. Of course these children will be slower in starting to read but this will not imply that they are less able.

Large classes of forty children, which are unfortunately the rule these days, prevent the teacher from teaching reading on an individual basis. She has no choice but to aim her teaching at the majority of the class. This normally, but by no means always, covers children of average ability.

I will now examine the ingredients of a reading programme, the sort that might be drawn up for the average infants class throughout its stay in infants school.

111

11 Recommended books

Pre-readers or caption books

It is often the practice, before children are put on a reading scheme proper, to give them what are known as 'pre-readers'. These consist of simple books, usually with a picture and a short caption on each page. Occasionally they tell a story. They are cheaply produced, running to less than a dozen pages, with paper covers. In my opinion they make the best introduction to reading. I would prefer to see them used in place of all other forms of preparation for reading, such as flash cards and word-matching exercises. The procedure is for the teacher to read these caption books, first of all to the whole class, and then to each child individually. The class reading is simply to create interest, but the individual reading, when the teacher points to each word and gets the child to repeat the process, is teaching the mechanics as well as the meaning of reading. The teacher spends time looking at the pictures and discussing them with the child. It is obviously desirable for the pictures to be interesting and the print to be large, clear, and well-spaced. Aside from my personal preference for this way of beginning reading, it must be considered the most efficient approach in a 'family grouped' classroom, where the age range is from five to nearly eight years. The advantage here is that it avoids the need for the teacher to start afresh a basic reading programme with each small batch of newcomers.

The publishing firm of Methuen built their new reading

scheme on the principle of caption books used in this way. In this respect Methuen's is an admirable scheme in its early stages, although the quality of the caption books is variable. I hope this example will encourage teachers to use caption books properly and not as many do, as incidental library material.

An ideal source of pre-reader material is at hand in the form of nursery rhymes. A familiar nursery rhyme arranged as a caption book, i.e. one line per page, would give the young beginning reader an immediate sense of achievement. There are plenty of nursery rhyme books about, but their layout is unsuitable for learners. Understandably nursery rhyme collections try to be comprehensive. However well designed, they are principally meant for adults to read to children. The nearest thing to my suggestion that I have seen, is an attractive new series of pre-readers called 'Stories the Rhymes Tell' published by Basil Blackwell.

Because there are a great many pre-readers I can recommend quite a long list of them. At the same time I cannot pretend it will be exhaustive. The following books have all passed the test of popularity with the children, helping to ease them into the reading programme:

Title	Author	Publisher
'Stories the Rhymes Tell' series	D. V. Thackray and Lucy Thackray	Basil Blackwell
'This is the Way I Go' series	Jenny Taylor and Terry Ingleby	Longmans
'Butch Books' series	Peter and Marilyn Lejeune	Cassell
I Can Read	Dick Bruna	Methuen
'Ready Steady Rhythm Readers' red set	(art work by Victor Ward)	Holmes McDougall
The Methuen Caption Books		
The Red Books plus the Yellow, Blue, and Green Books	Beverly Randell and Conrad Frieboe	Methuen
The Purple and Orange books	Beverly Randell and Jill McDonald	Methuen

Title	Author	Publisher
'The Read it Yourself Books' series	June Mesler	Methuen
'Let's Read' series	Vera Card and Monica Walker	Holmes McDougall
*Ladybird Learning to Read Books Series 563 'The Party' 'The Zoo' 'Telling the Time' 'Going to School' and others	M. E. Gagg	Wills and Hepworth
'First Words' series	Vera Southgate	Macmillan
'Little Picture Books' series	L. G. Studman and Harry Grice	Warne
'Looking at Words' series	Mollie Clarke	Rupert Hart-Davis

*This series is quite distinct from The Ladybird Reading Scheme

As will be seen, pre-readers are generally available in sets with rather functional and uninspiring names. However the titles of the individual books within a set are often more evocative. For example 'The Ladybird Learning to Read' series 563 includes 'The Party', 'The Zoo' etc. The model series is perhaps 'This is the Way I Go' written by Jenny Taylor and Terry Ingleby. Among the titles are 'I Can Fly', 'I Can Swim', 'I Can Crawl'. These books are completely successful through bright, clear, and colourful pictures integrated with the text, which provides repetition without loss of interest. The way in which a new word is identified by the picture on each page is shown by the example of 'I Can Fly'. The pictures in this book are of creatures which can fly. On each page the same statement is repeated for the appropriate creature, e.g. 'I can fly' said the butterfly, 'I can fly' said the bird, and so on. The book closes as do the others in the series, with a suitable little puzzle: a picture of several creatures among which the reader has to spot the one which cannot fly.

Another excellent series is 'The Butch Books' which recount

the adventures of a dog named Butch. The success of this set comes from its bold and simple illustrations and its story line. The superiority of books like these comes from their more subtle use of phrases and sentences, rather than simply nouns, as captions. This makes them more useful for teaching the fundamentals of reading. It is not too difficult to bring nouns into early reading because, for the most part, they lend themselves to illustration although their usefulness is limited. The value of a series like the 'This is the Way I Go' books is that at one and the same time they introduce rare and unfamiliar words which are interesting and exciting, and get repetition for plainer more useful words as an incidental benefit. After reading the series there is a good chance that such basic words as 'I', 'can', 'said', and 'the' will be painlessly embedded in the child's memory, even though the more exciting individual words may have been forgotten.

Graded readers

While there is a reasonable choice of pre-readers, the next stage of reading, in theory covering the introduction of the graded reader, presents an abysmal selection. This is not to say there are not plenty of schemes, each of which has its beginning books. Unfortunately the beginning of a reading scheme usually shows it in its worst aspects, although there are one or two exceptions which I shall mention later.

My experience has convinced me that the general run of graded reader could be dispensed with altogether and that it would be much more sensible to cast one's net as widely as possible to come up with an assortment of books that could be graded by the teacher or the head. Regrettably this task is beyond the resources of many teachers. They lack the time, and in most schools, the choice of books. There is no doubt that a really well thought-out graded reading scheme, possessing a far wider repertoire and appeal than the existing ones would be the best answer. Many teachers and especially new teachers, need the reassurance of a scheme so that they can quickly and easily keep track of the children's progress.

Let me make it clear that what I am in favour of is more grading rather than less grading, providing it is flexible and related to the needs of a range of children. I do not hold with the school of thought that favours doing away with all grading. This I am afraid is idealistic and impractical.

The only graded reader that I can wholeheartedly recommend at this stage is the 'One, Two, Three and Away!' series by S. K. McCullagh. These books contain ingeniously amusing stories, with jolly characters who are ageless and classless, and who belong to various families distinguished by the colour of their hats. They have real adventures right from the start. The series has now been expanded to include four introductory readers and supplementary readers for the first four books in the series. It is still too steep for average and backward beginners and by the time Book 5 is reached – 'The Cat's Dance' – the text to picture ratio and the style of the text make it more appropriate for juniors. I can therefore recommend it only as far as Book 4.

Because of the shortage of good material in the category of first readers I include with some hesitation the first books of two further reading schemes. They are the Ladybird and the Methuen schemes. Ladybird starts well but quickly peters out and the Methuen series is good in patches. It is fortunate that a lot of children will make a fairly quick transition to the next more expansive stage of reading. There are those that fall by the wayside who could be helped by more first readers. I suggest more pot boiling with pre-readers until, hopefully, publishers bring out more suitable books to bridge this important gap.

My recommendations are the following:

Title	Author	Publisher
'One, Two, Three and Away!' series (up to Book 4)	S. K. McCullagh	Rupert Hart-Davis
'Animal Books' series	Helen Piers	Methuen
'Gay Colour Books'	Alice Williamson and Sylvia M. Leach	E. J. Arnold
'Tom Cat' series	Mollie Clarke	Collins

Title	*Author*	*Publisher*
'Ready Steady Rhythm Readers' Yellow books	(art work by Victor Ward)	Holmes McDougall
Ladybird Key Words scheme (up to Book 3)	W. Murray and J. McNally	Wills and Hepworth

When a child has to begin to help himself

The next stage of reading is when the reading vocabulary is beginning to grow to a level above which the reader will not be able to teach every word and the child will have to begin to help himself. Children who are being taken through a single reading scheme find extreme difficulty at this point because, although they have been able to memorize the vocabulary of previous books from flash card work, they cannot cope with the rate of increase of new words. The conventional answer is further constraint on these children to slow them down, to get them to do more preparation in the shape of memorizing of words or through phonic drill. This can only delay their acquisition of a working vocabulary. The way round this difficulty is a change of reading scheme which will often restimulate the flagging child. Fortunately at the stage of reading we are discussing there are a number of books, including selected titles from various series, which can give the required changes of style and pace. Since most reading schemes are too steeply graded for the average child it is helpful if the teacher mixes books from series and individual titles in order to make for a more gentle gradient. The best tonic for jaded young readers is to be found in the 'I Can Read it all by Myself' Beginner Books. Among these titles there are some with a vocabulary under a hundred words, one or two as small as fifty words, of which they make the best possible use with funny and ingenious stories such as 'Go Dog Go' and 'Green Eggs and Ham'. They have all the virtues that we have stressed. They have a small amount of text per page, the illustrations keep the story going at a rattling pace, and they are quickly read. Without doubt they are the best of readers and the children's favourites. The fact that they are hard-backed and comparatively expensive should not stop them being used as readers. Children feel it is a treat to be given a grander style of book from time to time. I have never known any child react unfavourably to these books and the pity is there are so few of them at this stage.

A controversy about social class

The rest of the material is subdued in comparison but there are a number of attractive titles. The Nipper series edited by Leila Berg has aroused interest to the point of controversy and even of shocking some teachers. It is worth a digression to examine some of the issues raised by this bold new attempt. As often happens, a superficial controversy has obscured both the merits and the drawbacks of the series. What is all the fuss about? The publishers claim that the Nipper series is a 'deliberate attempt to provide first class stories for children particularly those from ordinary homes. They give the children the chance to read about themselves'.

The intention to produce first class stories is admirable and by and large has been carried out. 'Nippers' are not specifically meant as reading primers, although they are graded for children from six to eight years. They act as supplementary readers and can be used only by established readers. Such children will have moved away from the period of getting pleasure from self-identification which is found in the age group three to six years. With these younger children pleasure in self-identification can be exploited by the teacher and used as a ploy to create interest where the vocabulary is too small to sustain a story. Then why do the creators of Nippers series feel that children need to read about themselves? Children from the age of six have adventurous tastes and they love fantasy above everything. They genuinely love to read about characters of such social standing as Kings, Queens, Princes, Princesses, and Knights. Certainly they are a long way from seeking social realism. I believe that Leila Berg and her colleagues, in reacting against the middle-class characters and situations of

118

conventional readers, have somewhat missed the point. It is the priggishness of the characters and not their social class as such that bores and irritates young readers. One is also forced to ask how the publishers arrived at their definition of an 'ordinary home'. It appears to be no less than a city slum. Although far too many people do live in city slums, they are only a minority of the population, and so this ordinary home must be alien to many children. One book, set in a slum-dwelling with a leaking roof, and called 'Fish and Chips for Supper' succeeds because it is a good story, and because the drips from the roof are funny, not because children identify with the hole in their own roof. Another example 'The Key' falls down because the story is slight and the real 'latch key kids' I have observed, remain uninterested in a story aimed directly at them. Most of the other stories in the series are good but children's authors should beware that stories about working-class children can be just as dull as those about any other kind of children. Children of this age know no snobbery either of the real or inverted kind.

My recommended list therefore consists of the following:

Title	Author	Publisher
'I Can Read it all by Myself'		Collins
Beginner Books		
Go Dog Go	P. D. Eastman	
Green Eggs and Ham	Dr Seuss	
Put me in the Zoo	Robert Lopshire	
Ten Apples up on Top	Theo Le Sieg	
Come over to my House	Theo Le Sieg	
Snow	P. D. Eastman and Roy McKie	
Janet and John Story Books Blue Group numbers 11–15	Miriam Blanton Huber, Frank Seely Salisbury, and Mabel O'Donnell	Nisbet

(Note that the 'Janet and John' Story Books do not feature Janet and John themselves but are traditional tales.)

Title	Author	Publisher
Nippers Red series and Orange series	edited by Leila Berg	Macmillan
Griffin Pirate Stories (Books 1–4)	S. K. McCullagh	E. J. Arnold
Reading with Rhythm series	Jenny Taylor and Terry Ingleby	Longmans
'Ready Steady Rhythm Readers' Green books	(art work by Victor Ward)	Holmes McDougall

Books for fluent learners

My next selection represents books which contain a much wider vocabulary and are generally more difficult, while remaining within the grasp of children who have come to read fluently the type of book I last mentioned.

The Red and Black Rhyme book is notable for its novel format. The 'red and black' refer to the fact that the rhymes are printed partly in red and partly in black type. The teacher can read one colour of print and the child the other. The rhymes are well chosen and the book is justifiably popular on account of the teacher participation, which allows a more difficult vocabulary to be tackled. Finally the book is also a favourite because one or two of the rhymes have verbal traps, which the children never tire of falling into.

Benn's 'Beginning to Read' books and the Muller 'Easy Reading' series are both sets of more substantial hard-backed books, probably intended for class libraries. Nonetheless they make better reading material than most of that in graded reading schemes. The outstanding titles are 'The Curious Cow', 'Oh Essie', and 'Tim's Giant Marrow', from Benn's series and 'The Boy who fooled the Giant' from Muller's.

My earlier remarks about the Collins 'I Can Read it all by Myself' series hold good for the next grouping of readers. They are still the best and most effective of all available reading material at this stage. There are no duds among the many titles. Perhaps the children's favourite is 'I Wish that I had Duck Feet' which pushes the notorious 'Cat in the Hat' into second place.

RECOMMENDED BOOKS

The range of titles produced by the World's Work Press comprises my second choice of the very best books for this reading group. They are uniformly excellent, with humour as their strong point. Although they are 'expensive' hard-back books they are unquestionably worth their place in a general reading programme. Children's special favourites include 'The Little Bear' books, 'Sammy the Seal', 'Grizzwold', 'Hurry Hurry', and 'Stop Stop'. My recommendations are these:

Title	Author	Publisher
'I Can Read it All by Myself' Beginner Books		Collins
The Cat in the Hat	Dr Seuss	
A Fly Went By	Mike McClintock	
The Big Jump	Benjamin Elkin	
Sam and The Firefly	P. D. Eastman	
A Fish Out of Water	Helen Palmer	
Robert the Rose Horse	Joan Heilbroner	
Summer	Alice Low	
The Big Honey Hunt	S. and J. Berenstein	
The King The Mice and the Cheese	N. and E. Gurney	
I Wish that I had Duck Feet	Theo Le Sieg	
The Bike Lesson	S. and J. Berenstein	
Hugh Lofting's Travels of Dr Dolittle	Al Perkins	
I Can Read books		World's Work Press
The Fire Cat	Esther Averill	
Hurry Hurry	Edith Thacher Hurd	
Stop Stop	Edith Thacher Hurd	
Who's a Pest	Crosby Bonsall	
No Funny Business	Edith Thacher Hurd	

Title	Author	Publisher
Stanley	Syd Hoff	
Grizzwold	Syd Hoff	
The Case of the Hungry Stranger	Crosby Bonsall	
Little Bear	Else Homelund Minarik	
Little Bear's Friend	Else Homelund Minarik	
Little Bear's Visit	Else Homelund Minarik	
Julius	Syd Hoff	
Sammy the Seal	Syd Hoff	
Oliver	Syd Hoff	
The Red and Black Rhyme Book	J. Gibson and R. Wilson	Macmillan
Janet and John Story Books Pink Group 21–28	Miriam Blanton Huber, Frank Seely Salisbury, and Mabel O'Donnell	Nisbet
The Pancake	These make up	Ginn & Co.
The Wise Little Goat	Beacon Book	
The Dragon Princess	Three and supplementaries	
Nippers (Yellow series)	Edited by Leila Berg	Macmillan
Ladybird Series 606d Well Loved Tales	Various authors	Wills and Hepworth
Muller's 'Easy Reading' Series	Various authors	Muller
Benn's Beginning to Read books	Various authors	Benn
First Folk Tales	Mollie Clarke	Rupert Hart-Davis
Turnip Tales	Malcom Joseph	Basil Blackwell

My next group of books would take children to a point where they would have no need of reading schemes or of grading at all. The so-called 'extension readers' provided with certain reading schemes are quite superfluous. Children who reach this stage still

need help and supervision in choosing books to read both from
school and public libraries. I fear this is not automatic in certain
schools where once a child has reached a certain proficiency in
reading, anything but functional reading is ignored. However
short of space, every school should provide a library.

Recommendations:

Title	Author	Publisher
'Starting to Read Books'		
Noggin the Nog 1–6	Oliver Postgate and Peter Firmin	Edmund Ward
Basil Brush 7–8	Peter Firmin	Edmund Ward
Careful Hans	These make up	Ginn & Co.
Annancy Stories	Beacon Book 4 and	
The Faithful Beast	supplementaries	
Briar Rose	These make up	Ginn & Co.
The Emperor's New Clothes	Beacon Book 5 and	
The Seven Proud Sisters	supplementaries	
Dragon Pirate Stories	S. K. McCullagh	E. J. Arnold
Cowboy Sam Books	Edna Walker Chandler	E. J. Arnold
Bruna Books	Dick Bruna	Methuen
Bod Books	Michael and Joanne Cole	Methuen
Janet and John Story Books Maroon Group 31–39	Miriam Blanton Huber, Frank Seely Salisbury, and Mabel O'Donnell	Nisbet
Nippers Green and Blue series	Edited by Leila Berg	Macmillan

Balancing reading age and actual age

For children who have made slow progress and are perhaps
eight years old or more by the time they are making any
headway with reading, some of the previously listed books will
appear babyish. There is still a choice of good reading schemes
for such children. In addition to the ones I have listed below I
would continue to press the claims of the Collins Beginner books
and the World's Work Press books.

Title	Author	Publisher
The Griffin Pirate Stories	S. K. McCullagh	E. J. Arnold
The Dragon Books	S. K. McCullagh	E. J. Arnold
Sea Hawk Books	S. K. McCullagh	E. J. Arnold
Adventures in Space	S. K. McCullagh	Rupert Hart-Davis

E. J. Arnold seems to be the publisher most conscious of possible discrepancies between reading age and actual age. As far as I know, they and Methuens are the only publishers making use in their catalogues of a system suggested by the Publishers Association which codes books with reference to both reading ability and the interests appropriate to physical age. Numbers denote the reading ability groups and letters the interest ranges. For example the Griffin Pirate Stories and the Dragon Pirate stories that I have mentioned above, are both catalogued as 2BCD. This means that they will be suitable for children with a reading age of 6–8 years and an interest age between 6–12 years. One hopes this useful system is quickly adopted by all publishers and that they will take the trouble to spell out the reading age and interest age involved to provide a guide for both teachers and parents.

An example of the age problem is the otherwise commendable Dick Bruna series. These books are of stylized simplicity but the vocabulary is sometimes far from simple. For this reason they are included in my final group of recommendations, although they are likely to grate on children, particularly boys, above seven years of age, although they remain excellent books for children who are ready for them before the age of seven. Dick Bruna has produced a lot of titles and has created a unique style for both traditional tales and his own inventions such as 'The King', 'The Egg', 'Miffy', 'The Circus'. Dick Bruna's art is to strip stories to their bare essentials, so making them excellent for reading aloud to very young children.

Both the Noggin the Nog books and the Basil Brush books are based on TV characters and are especially popular on that account. However they easily stand by themselves as well-written and entertaining stories.

The books I have listed, some of them top-rate and all of them good, lend themselves to use as graded reading material. The gradings as indicated are entirely my own and are not meant to be rigid. Give or take one or two titles there is a reasonable precision about them. Also I have left out books that I know are good but which are not included because the text is too difficult simply for the purposes of reading alone. However, there are plenty of books which are useful at this age, for browsing through, for dipping into, or for reading aloud by a grown-up.

12 Reading resolutions

We live in a society where advertising men, who should know, classify teachers as skilled workers. Perhaps this is no bad thing. Teachers now seem to have decided to accept their more workaday status and to press for the financial rewards skilled workers are accustomed to getting. They are ceasing to think of themselves as distressed gentlefolk. Meanwhile the methods and institutions in which teachers are trained have come in for heavy criticism. Their narrowness and unpracticality have been attacked. People are finding it strange that engineers and classicists, metallurgists and biologists, are allowed to mingle in university, but future teachers are kept quite separate, in the manner of handmaidens. All thinking teachers, and on the whole teachers are a thoughtful lot, must now be sizing up their role, their status, and their methods. I hope my book will make a contribution to this educational debate for I believe it is essential the revaluation should come from working teachers rather than be imposed from above by technical administrators.

In infants teaching, which is by far the most advanced area of education, and in the teaching of reading in particular, overly technical solutions can be a bugbear. In the first place teachers know that all relevant techniques work to some extent, particularly in their experimental phase. An atmosphere of anxious and possibly competitive enthusiasm is set up which tends to produce the desired result, but there is no follow up to see what happens when all the fuss has died down. Patience and the ability to

126

follow through are the teacher's strengths. A great deal of patience is needed to deal with merely fashionable advice, for example to 'enrich the children's spoken vocabulary' by studied conversation, as an essential preparation for reading. Any teacher, and any parent come to that, knows that the problem with small children is not to get them to talk but to get them to shut up! On the face of it the suggestion appears as an attempt to break down the separation between the vernacular and literary languages. If it means learning 'big words' prior to reading and giving working class children a middle class vocabulary, in practice it does not work. Children find it difficult to retain words that are artificially induced but when they come across them naturally in the course of their reading they are much more likely to stick. The other main danger of technical panaceas, accompanied by all the paraphernalia of statistical proof, is that they defer the basic and serious problem of staff shortage. If you are presented with dramatic evidence that a new method, i.t.a. say, is remarkably more efficient than existing methods, the implication is obvious that there will be an improvement in education even without a reduction in class sizes.

The teachers' plea for smaller classes is unfortunately more than a slogan for a better life. As far as learning to read is concerned, the time factor is vital. Very slow readers and borderline cases would be brought back from failure quite easily if only there were enough time for personal supervision and coaching. In any case, in teaching children to read we are not concerned simply with bringing the maximum number to an acceptable threshold. The aim must be to get children to read and to enjoy reading, as the basis of all their education, as soon as is practically and psychologically possible. With less able children we have to concentrate on avoiding the embarrassment and resentment that comes from failure in what has been seen as the stern duty of reading. In the end it all comes down to some very simple things, good reading books, good teachers, and interested parents. I hope my book will encourage them.

My purpose has been to generate confidence, first of all

self-confidence in teachers to build up their own repertoire of ideas, methods, and materials, and confidence among parents that in the infant classroom their children will be educated and made happy as individuals. I have also asked teachers and parents to be alert to the dangers of obsolete, timid, and careless ways. If I have been occasionally scathing about well-intentioned people and products it has been to point up the crucial importance of a discriminating approach. I have tried not to appear a reading fanatic. Indeed I feel the greatest stimulus to education can come from the interaction of media, especially between TV and print. For instance the craze for whales in one of my classes of five-year-olds was started by a TV programme. Then all the books on the sea which had been more or less ignored, were feverishly scanned, and the children became walking encyclopaedias on whales. I do happen to believe that learning to read is very much bound up with the way children learn to think and feel as individuals. That is why it deserves great care, and continuing respect for children's own likes and dislikes.